RAND

Virtual Team Success

Virtual Team Success

Success

A Practical Guide for Working and Leading from a Distance

Darleen M. DeRosa

Richard Lepsinger

JOSSEY-BASS
A Wiley Imprint
www.josseybass.com

Published by Jossey-Bass
A Wiley Imprint
989 Market Street, San Francisco, CA 94103-1741—www.josseybass.com

Jossey-Bass books and products are available through most bookstores. To contact Jossey-Bass directly call our Customer Care Department within the U.S. at 800-956-7739, outside the U.S. at 317-572-3986, or fax 317-572-4002.

Jossey-Bass also publishes its books in a variety of electronic formats. Some content that appears in print may not be available in electronic books.

Library of Congress Cataloging-in-Publication Data

DeRosa, Darleen M., 1970-
    Virtual team success : a practical guide for working and leading from a distance / Darleen M. DeRosa and Richard Lepsinger. — 1st ed.
        p. cm.
    Includes bibliographical references and index.
    ISBN 978-0-470-53296-6 (cloth)
    ISBN 978-0-470-77059-7 (ebk)
    ISBN 978-0-470-87240-6 (ebk)
    ISBN 978-0-470-87241-3 (ebk)
  1. Virtual work teams. I. Lepsinger, Richard, 1948- II. Title.
    HD66.D466 2010
    658.4'022—dc22

                                                                                    2010019248

Printed in the United States of America
FIRST EDITION
HB Printing 10 9 8 7 6 5 4 3 2

To my husband Joe and son Andrew; to my parents,
Michael and Marianna, who always provided endless love
and support; and my grandmother, Tina, who taught me
the importance of perseverance.
—D.D.

To Bonnie, with love.
—R.L.

Contents

List of Tables, Case Studies, Figures, and Exhibits

Acknowledgments

We are grateful to many people for their help and support during the writing of this book. In particular we'd like to thank:

Jessica Lipnack and Jeffrey Stamps, whose insightful books and articles on virtual teams were a major source of inspiration to conduct work in this area. Angela Travagline, who partnered with us throughout the research study and provided valuable insights that helped shape the book. Donald Hantula and Ned Kock, who collaborated with us on several research studies and articles that were a catalyst for our applied research.

Our business partner, Jennifer Forgie, whose suggestions and feedback were invaluable in helping refine and focus the chapters. Max Wolfe whose research and data gathering where tremendously helpful.

The companies, virtual team members, team leaders, and various stakeholders who participated in OnPoint's global research study. Their time and commitment added richness to the cases, examples, and guidelines that make up the book.

The people who are experts at working from a distance who generously shared their stories and experiences: Laszlo Bock, Mark Feurer, Mark Gasta, Jay Moldenhauer- Salazar, Karen O'Boyle, Kevin Squires, Swroop Sahota, Cleo Stockhoff, and Theresa Zeller.

Dottie DeHart and her team at DeHart & Company, who partnered with us to enhance the book's content and readability.

And last, but certainly not least, to our spouses. To Joe DeRosa, who was a pillar of strength during the seemingly endless writing process. To Bonnie Uslianer, who endured months of being a "book widow" while providing unconditional support and encouragement.

Foreword

When Darleen asked us to write the foreword to her book, we were immediately inclined to do so. With a Ph.D. in organizational psychology for which she wrote a dissertation on virtual teams and subsequently having conducted two substantial research studies on the topic as a management consultant, she has the bona fides to write authoritatively on the subject.

That Darleen and her co-author and business partner, Rick Lepsinger, have chosen to tackle the sore spot of virtual teams—why they fail—is testament to their expertise, energy, and insight.

A decade ago, Darleen's earliest work in this field was a research study of how "naturally" virtual teams perform over time using different kinds of media. While the technology studied then seems primitive by today's standards, her foresight in tackling this topic when few others were considering it is laudable. Technology, she concluded, plays a role, but other factors in real work settings may prove equally or more important.

She continued her work in the putative "real world" as a management consultant, teaming up with Rick, and ultimately leading to this comprehensive examination of what trips up virtual teams and what leaders can do about it.

Here you will find numerous research-based "devices" for clearing the hurdles that virtual teams present. It's not enough in a 24/7 global work environment to take the old face-to-face techniques and apply them when people are not co-located. Failed projects and missed deadlines in countless organizations indicate that we need new ways to work. The demands of contemporary work environments—distributed, asynchronous, multicultural, and without the benefit of hallway time—require us to think—and behave—differently.

The many frameworks, guidelines, checklists, and recommendations in this book will make life easier for the newest managers, those leading virtual teams. There's no school for this yet, but when the first is established, *Virtual Team Success: A Practical Guide for Working and Leading from a Distance* will certainly be the core curriculum.

—Jessica Lipnack and Jeffrey Stamps, authors of *Virtual Teams, The Age of the Network,* and many other books

Introduction

"We have modified our environment so radically
that we must modify ourselves in order to exist in
this new environment."

—*Norbert Wiener,*
The Human Use of Human Beings[1]

"If there is an office in the future," wrote Charles Handy in a
1995 *Harvard Business Review* article[2] on virtual work, "it will be
more like a clubhouse: a place for meeting, eating, and greeting,
with rooms reserved for activities, not for particular people."
Admittedly, most organizations haven't reached that point yet,
but the way we work has certainly changed dramatically since
Handy's mid-1990s predictions. Today, some organizations have
created "hotelling" options for employees, in which they no
longer have assigned offices, and it is increasingly common to
leverage telecommuting and virtual teamwork.

To put this brave new world in context, consider the fact that
in the late 1980s and early 1990s, few people had heard of virtual
teams. At that time only a small number of companies were even
using them. Today, of course, companies big and small are using
some form of virtual collaboration.

Many of the nation's major corporations are choosing to go
virtual. According to a study from *Communications of the ACM*[3]
(conducted by Intel Corporation in April 2009) approximately
two-thirds of the company's employees were on virtual teams.
Jay Moldenhauer-Salazar, who is currently the vice president

of Talent Management at Gap, Inc., and formerly held senior HR roles in Sun Microsystems, Taco Bell, and Barclays Global Investors, estimates that virtual teams are used to deliver projects about 50 percent of the time at Sun and BGI. Similarly, Laszlo Bock, vice president of People Operations at Google, states that at least 50 percent of Google employees are working on virtual teams at any given time.

Virtual collaboration has already begun to transform many business sectors. For example, it's becoming increasingly used in the health care industry because it helps to improve availability and treatment. A January 2007 *Financial Times* article illustrates those benefits. It discusses the use of virtual teams during the Amazon Swim Project, a geographically dispersed team of researchers who were assisting a marathon swimmer as he swam almost 3,500 miles. Using advanced medical technology, the team provided health care services for the swimmer and his support team. By collaborating virtually, the medical team was able to include the best specialists and experts from all over the globe.

Another great example is Virtual Integrated Practice (VIP), a health care delivery model developed by Rush University Medical Center in Chicago. The program is designed to address the challenges of caring for elderly and chronically ill patients, who commonly have complex needs.

VIP develops effective team building and ongoing collaboration among health care providers who are not in the same locations or even in the same organizations. It prevents the logistical obstacles of having clinicians meet in person to discuss patient cases by providing a system that allows them to meet "virtually." The two-year study yielded positive results. When VIP was used, there were fewer emergency room visits and increased patient awareness. Physicians on the VIP team were also more informed about patient progress than those who were not on the team.

Why Virtual Teams Are More Prevalent

So what has contributed to this dramatic shift in the way people work, and more specifically, the growing popularity of virtual workplaces? At least in part it has been the gradual shift of the U.S. economy from manufacturing and production to one of knowledge and information. But there are three other important reasons.

First, organizations are looking for the best available talent, regardless of their geographic location, which has led them to use virtual collaboration. Today, when forming teams, rather than rely on a group of people who are geographically closer but may not have the right expertise, many companies strategically select talented individuals who have the appropriate skill set, even though they may live thousands of miles apart.

Bock at Google reports that "one of the biggest drivers of virtual teamwork is that we believe that there are talented people everywhere in the world, so we have numerous locations in order to access talent. We do a lot of remote work and collaboration. For example, most of our engineering teams span three continents."

Theresa Zeller, executive director/leader, GHH Marketing Learning at Merck, states, "We work in a global environment and our clients are geographically distributed, so it doesn't matter if our team is in one place. If you have a global mindset, time and distance become irrelevant. In a lean and flexible organization where your expertise is needed globally, we need to be able to conduct business in a global manner while enhancing efficiency."

In 2007, IBM's effort to become a "globally integrated enterprise" gained significant momentum. Historically, IBM had created mini versions of itself in each country where it operated, which was inefficient and expensive. Today, as a "globally integrated enterprise" the company just sets up shop wherever it finds the right talent at the right price. For example, global IT service delivery in India, global supply chain in China, and global financing back office in Brazil.

Bottom line: The use of virtual teams better enables organizations to leverage talented employees without having to bring them together face-to-face.

The second reason for the prevalence of virtual teams is that the emergence of a global economy has made it particularly challenging for organizations to quickly capitalize on shifts in the marketplace and bring new products to market, effectively innovate, and respond to customers' needs. Having team members in various locations around the world enables organizations to better meet these challenges.

For example, Merck's global pharmaceutical research and development teams capitalize on having dispersed team members who are able to continuously work together on different initiatives. Essentially, they are a global R&D dream team. Team members in Asia start on a project and, when their day ends, they pass their work on to team members in the United States, whose work picks up where their Asia-based teammates left off. By enabling this "work relay." Merck is able to extend work hours and, in turn, enhance its productivity, flexibility, and innovation.

Using virtual teams can also be a huge benefit to an organization's clients. In fact, one global consulting firm leverages virtual project teams to deliver solutions to its clients. Rather than simply drawing on local talent in one area, the organization can call on teams throughout the world and tap into their thought leadership based on the nature of the work. This allows the firm to have many varying points of view contributing and as much creative input as possible on each project, which enhances the service they provide their clients and ensures that clients receive high-quality solutions in a very efficient way.

The third reason for the growing popularity of virtual workplaces? Technology. There's no denying that advances in technology now allow organizations to achieve greater levels of efficiency and cost savings. And every year new technologies are introduced to make it even easier and more efficient for globally dispersed teams to work together no matter how far they are physically from one another.

In a November 2008 *Harvard Business Review* article,[4] John Chambers, the CEO of Cisco, discussed using TelePresence technology to conduct a team meeting with individuals from Beijing, Frankfurt, New Delhi, Kuwait, and San Jose. Chambers asserted, "What might have taken us days before took us just fifteen minutes, and we were able to make decisions out of this short single session."

TelePresence, which is a sophisticated high-definition video-conferencing technology, allows virtual team members to hold meetings and feel as though they are sitting across a conference room table from one another, rather than just hearing a voice on the telephone or IMing a person in a chat room. The technology seems to far surpass the quality of traditional videoconferencing tools, and perhaps most importantly, enhances the connectivity of virtual teams.

In a June 2008 *BusinessWeek* article by Michelle Conlin on the demise of those diehard business travelers,[5] she calls "road warriors", she explains that CIOs who've used the program say that TelePresence, which carries a price tag of around $300,000, typically pays for itself within nine months. In the same article, Fillippo Passerini, Procter & Gamble's chief information officer, asserts that these new technologies "empower collaboration, so you really can be there without leaving here. They are saving money and enabling us to collaborate and innovate faster, smarter, and more sustainable than ever before."

It's obvious that working virtually is cost-effective for companies that regularly spend significant amounts of money hosting off-site meetings and paying travel expenses for routine face-to-face meetings. All that travel also results in decreased productivity and can lead to poor work/life balance, which impacts engagement and morale. Companies see the use of virtual teams as a way to reduce some of these costs and help employees better manage their time.

Karen O'Boyle, president of North America for DBM, a global outplacement, coaching, and career transition services firm, states that "speed and cost are both drivers of virtual teams and 80 percent of our internal work is now done through virtual teams."

In her *BusinessWeek* article, Conlin[6] provides an example of BDO Seidman, a consulting firm that saves more than $1 million annually due to virtual collaboration. And in Conlin's article, MaryEm Musser, the company's director of training and development, indicates that meeting virtually "is not just about travel reduction, it's also about increasing communication" because getting people together more frequently for short meetings is much more productive than sending them on long business trips.

In a 2003 *Stanford Business* article, Bill Snyder[7] discusses the challenges John Monroe, a senior executive at Hewlett-Packard, faced when travel budgets were cut and his team had a large, complex initiative and needed to work virtually. In short, Monroe and his team, which included team members in sixteen different countries, exceeded expectations. In fact, they saved the company $1 million a year in compliance and cycle time costs.

Already showing a positive impact for big-time companies, these technologies will likely continue to get better and better, further enhancing virtual collaboration. Certain social networking sites have already been adapted for use in a business setting. Companies such as IBM and BP use Second Life, which is a 3-D environment where users can collaborate and learn. And at IBM, for example, employees use it to "meet" on a private island that IBM owns in Second Life.

But it should be said that, while new technologies certainly enable virtual team collaboration, technology should be viewed as one piece of a larger puzzle, rather than the "be all, end all" solution. Despite the optimism that improved technologies will continue to emerge over time, organizations will always need to balance their use of these technologies with the interpersonal and collaborative processes necessary to support virtual teamwork.

In a 2008 study conducted by our company, OnPoint Consulting, we found that many companies that had made significant investments in technology and virtual teams were not performing to their full potential due to ineffective team leadership, lack of accountability among team members, lack of time to focus on the team, and lack of skill training.

In fact the study found that more than 25 percent of the virtual teams were not performing up to par. The cause, we believe, is that organizations are approaching working on and leading virtual teams as if the dynamics are the same as those of team members who are working in the same location. By and large, companies do not take the steps necessary to ensure their virtual teams and their virtual team leaders are set up for success.

How the Book Is Organized

Until now, there has not been a resource available to guide organizations in setting up and getting the most out of virtual teams or to help virtual team members and leaders enhance their effectiveness collaborating or leading from a distance. The objective of this book is to fill that gap and provide a hands-on, practical toolkit for both members and leaders of virtual teams.

The book's overview of issues facing virtual teams and leaders and our recommendations to enhance virtual team performance come from two sources. First, we highlight the findings from our 2008 global research study on virtual teams. Forty-eight intact virtual teams from sixteen organizations spanning a variety of industries participated in the study, in which we looked at the factors that set top performing virtual teams apart from those that were average and below average. (*Note:* This book does not focus on the technical aspects of the study; however, if you are interested in the details, you can find additional information in the Appendix.)

In addition to the information included from our study, we also provide practical examples and insights throughout the book based on the more than fifty interviews we conducted with HR executives, members of virtual teams, virtual team leaders, and employees who have worked on virtual teams.

While this book can certainly be read from cover to cover, we recommend that you also use it as your go-to guide for working in and managing virtual teams. At any given time, just turn directly to the section you need most and get to work! For example, if you are on a virtual team, you might flip straight to the sections that discuss collaborating from a distance. Or, if you are leading a virtual team, you may want to skip to the sections that pertain specifically to leading from a distance.

We have also included applied tools that we've used in our consulting work. For example, the book includes several case study–like "brain teasers" that allow you to consider how you would handle certain challenging situations related to collaborating or leading from a distance. After you've finished reading the tips and guidelines related to those case studies, we recommend revisiting these real-world brain teasers to determine how you might respond differently based on what you've learned. In addition, we have also provided self-assessments, checklists, and other practical resources to enhance your team and individual effectiveness.

If you are a member of a virtual team, are leading a virtual team, or are responsible for ensuring the success of virtual teamwork, then this book will be a critical resource for you. Human resource professionals, executives, and leaders in information technology (IT), research and development (R&D), supply chain management, and anyone who uses geographically dispersed teams will also benefit from the applied recommendations covered in each section.

Section One focuses on the skills and characteristics necessary for building high performing virtual teams. Chapter One highlights our research findings on the challenges many virtual teams face and the pitfalls that often lead to failure. Chapter Two provides a profile of high-performing teams to outline what "good" looks like. Chapter Three is a practical toolkit and resource guide to help you successfully launch virtual teams. Chapter Four reviews the differentiators of successful virtual teams and introduces a practical model of top-performing teams. And we discuss strategies and tips that help team leaders and members boost virtual team performance.

Section Two focuses on best practices for leading from a distance. Chapter Five outlines our research findings on the unique leadership challenges that virtual team leaders face, and we discuss the practices of the most effective team leaders. Chapter Six addresses the critical things that virtual team leaders can do to boost the performance of virtual teams who are struggling to achieve their objectives. Chapter Seven is a practical guide for facilitating and managing virtual team communication. In it, we discuss tips for effectively facilitating virtual meetings and how to optimize technology use for virtual collaboration. Finally, the Conclusion summarizes some of the key lessons from our research and consulting work with virtual teams and team leaders.

Finding What You Need: A Quick Reference Guide

If you have a specific virtual team need or issue in mind, the following list of challenges and questions will help you quickly find the content you need.

Question/Challenge	Chapter
What are the factors that commonly derail virtual teams?	Chapter One
What are the characteristics that top-performing virtual teams share?	Chapter Two

Question/Challenge	Chapter
What are the best practices for successfully launching virtual teams?	Chapter Three
How can I build trust and reduce conflict in my virtual team?	Chapter Four
What can I do to motivate my virtual team?	Chapter Four
How can I enhance accountability in my virtual team?	Chapter Four and Chapter Five
How can I effectively manage change in a virtual environment?	Chapter Five
How can I enhance the level of cooperation and collaboration in my virtual team?	Chapter Five
How can I empower virtual team members?	Chapter Five
What differentiates the most effective virtual team leaders?	Chapter Five
How can I establish clear goals for virtual teamwork?	Chapter Five
How can I improve my virtual communication and facilitation skills?	Chapter Five and Chapter Seven
How can I better influence my virtual team members and more effectively gain their commitment to the team?	Chapter Six

Question/Challenge	Chapter
How can I learn the skills required to provide coaching and support for my virtual team?	Chapter Six
How can I boost virtual team performance?	Chapter Six
What steps can I take to hold virtual team members accountable?	Chapter Six
How can I recognize and reward virtual teams and their members?	Chapter Six
How can I conduct high-impact "v-meetings"?	Chapter Seven

We also provide assessments and checklists throughout the book that will allow you to gain a better understanding of your knowledge, skills, and leadership style in areas that are relevant to virtual teamwork. The following guide helps you find the assessments best suited to your needs.

Topic	Chapter
Test your virtual team launch IQ	Chapter Three
Discover the characteristics virtual team members and leaders need to work effectively in a virtual environment	Chapter Three
Determine whether your virtual team has a sense of purpose	Chapter Three

Topic	Chapter
Determine whether your organization will be able to support virtual teamwork	Chapter Three
Test your knowledge of how to enhance the performance of a virtual team that is experiencing challenges	Chapter Four
Diagnose your virtual team's performance issues and identify an appropriate solution	Chapter Four
Test your knowledge of how to enhance the performance of an average, but not great virtual team	Chapter Five
Assess your level of effectiveness leading virtual teams	Chapter Five
Assess your interpersonal communication skills	Chapter Five
Assess your delegation and empowerment skills	Chapter Five
Diagnose the leadership challenge your virtual team is facing and identify a solution	Chapter Five

We believe the common perception that virtual teams will never be as effective as traditional, face-to-face teams is false. Many companies we've worked with have already developed very successful strategies for working in virtual teams. Those companies, as well as our extensive research and consulting in this area, have given us many helpful insights and best practices. By sharing our findings in this book, we hope to empower you to help your organization create a successful and dynamic virtual environment.

Virtual Team Success

Section One

Building High-Performing
Virtual Teams

Chapter One

Why Virtual Teams Fail

"You have no choice but to operate in a world
shaped by globalization and the information
revolution. There are two options: Adapt or die. . . .
You need to plan the way a fire department plans. It
cannot anticipate fires, so it has to shape a flexible
organization that is capable of responding to
unpredictable events."

—*Andrew S. Grove, Intel Corporation*

Virtual teams are more prevalent than ever. It's not hard to see why. Advances in technology have made it easier to organize and manage dispersed groups of people. And competitive pressures and the needs of today's global market workforce have made virtual teams a necessity for some organizations.

Many companies are using virtual teams to reach business objectives and to get a leg up on their competition. However, in others, virtual teams are more opportunistic, emerging in response to a particular event or need. For example, joint ventures or acquisitions within the pharmaceutical industry have led to the use of virtual teams because different R&D functions need to collaborate to accomplish shared business goals.

But the fact that virtual teams continue to grow in popularity doesn't mean they're always being used and managed properly. Quite the contrary. When OnPoint started working with various organizations that used virtual teams, we noticed that few actually understood how to set their virtual teams up for success in order to ensure continued quality performance.

We found that many organizations simply recycled the same guidelines and best practices they were using for their co-located teams and hoped for the best. And frankly, that system wasn't working. It seemed obvious that face-to-face teams and virtual teams were the proverbial "apples and oranges" situation.

To help these organizations maximize their investment in virtual collaboration, we wanted to better understand what virtual teams need in order to consistently meet their performance expectations, and we wanted to uncover the unique obstacles these teams face.

So, in order to identify the specific practices associated with the most successful virtual teams and to better understand why some virtual teams fail, we conducted a study of forty-eight virtual teams across a broad range of industries. Three questions motivated our research:

- Why do many virtual teams fail to meet performance expectations?
- What differentiates the very best virtual teams from those that are less successful?
- What differentiates highly effective virtual team leaders from those that are less effective?

Keep in mind that we weren't using the study to compare face-to-face teams with virtual teams. Instead, we set out to understand what factors differentiate high-performing virtual teams from low-performing ones. We wanted to help so companies can implement specific high-impact strategies to make their virtual teams more productive.

As part of the study, we administered an online survey to 427 team members and leaders of intact virtual teams. (See the Appendix for demographics and study detail.) In addition, we collected third-party data from ninety-nine stakeholders—individuals who are very familiar with the teams, such as internal customers or the team leaders' managers—to objectively assess team performance.

And to better understand the common experiences and challenges for virtual team leaders and team members, we conducted more than fifty telephone interviews with virtual team members, team leaders, human resource (HR) professionals, and stakeholders. Plus, in a separate study, we administered an online survey to 304 individuals who worked on virtual teams but were not on the same team.

Given the prevalence of virtual teamwork, our research uncovered several factors that were cause for concern:

- In our study of the 304 individuals who worked on virtual teams, 25 percent reported that their teams were not fully effective.
- Third-party stakeholders who were familiar with a given team's performance were asked to rate its effectiveness. Of forty-eight teams, 27 percent were perceived to be adequate or below adequate in terms of their overall performance.
- When team members and team leaders were asked to assess their effectiveness, 17 percent of the teams rated their own performance as being adequate or below adequate.

The overall performance level of the teams seemed to be up for debate. When we looked at the gap between stakeholders' and team members' rating of the teams' performance levels, we found that there was a significant gap with one-third of the teams. For some of these teams, stakeholders rated team performance higher than team members, and for the remaining teams, stakeholders rated team performance lower than team members. These findings indicate that a significant number of virtual teams are not effective, and perhaps more importantly, that there is a gap in how team effectiveness is perceived that often goes undetected.

Key Challenges

In short, our research found that, while many virtual teams are successful, a significant number are not reaching their full potential. And based on gaps in the perception of team effectiveness, it also appears that many organizations are not even aware that their virtual teams are performing poorly.

A study discussed in the *MIT Sloan Management Review*[1] reinforces our findings. In that study, only 18 percent of the seventy global business virtual teams assessed were found to be highly successful. That means a whopping 82 percent did not achieve their goals!

But why are so many virtual teams falling into these performance traps? In order to answer this question and to better understand the challenges that virtual teams face, we asked hundreds of virtual team members and leaders to select the top three challenges that hinder their teams' performance. Table 1.1 outlines these results.

Perhaps not surprisingly, lack of face-to-face contact was cited as the top challenge. We found that the majority of virtual teams in our study reported meeting in-person only several times per year. However, we did find that lack of face-to-face contact was less of an issue for teams that had an initial face-to-face meeting

Table 1.1 Top Challenges of Virtual Teams

Challenges	Percentage of Responses
Lack of face-to-face contact with team members	46%
Lack of resources	37%
Time zone differences hinder our ability to collaborate	29%
Team members are on more than one team and cannot devote enough time to this team	27%
Team members do not share relevant information with one another	21%
Lack of skill training	20%

within the first thirty to ninety days of working virtually together. Overall, these teams were more effective than teams that had never met up-front.

We also examined whether teams had different challenges based on their level of effectiveness. Interestingly, all the teams in our study, regardless of their performance, reported the same top challenges. However, team members on low-performing teams also reported that their team members were on too many different teams, a factor that was unique to this population.

Several additional challenges were consistently mentioned in our interviews and have also been observed in our work with virtual teams. Surprisingly, team members—and in some cases team *leaders*—frequently lack clarity about who their fellow team members actually are.

That notion becomes less surprising, however, when you consider that many people reported that members of their teams changed monthly. With this common "revolving door" method for staffing teams, you can hardly blame them for not being able to keep up.

And having team members who are here today and gone tomorrow leads to another big challenge for virtual teams—*communication*. The frequent change of team members makes it difficult to find the most effective ways to communicate with one another and to build relationships effectively.

Add to that the fact that often people are invited to be on a given team solely because of political reasons, not because they are meant to contribute in a specific way. What you end up with, and what we found many organizations ended up with, are large virtual teams whose members don't have clear roles and who may not even know who their fellow team members are.

Now it's one thing not to know who your fellow team members are. Surely, though, if you are on a virtual team, you at least know who your leader is. Right? Wrong, actually. We found that in numerous instances team members were also unclear about who their team leader was (despite someone identifying him- or herself as the leader in these cases).

One explanation for these seemingly leaderless virtual teams could be the informal, often opportunistic way in which some virtual teams are formed.

In fact, virtual teams often come together out of nowhere. For example, one of our clients, a global consulting firm, came to the realization that, while the majority of its employees were working on virtual teams, no formal decision had ever been made to move in that direction.

In addition, frequent changes in team membership, a lack of formal on-boarding of new members, members who are simultaneously participating on different virtual teams, and infrequent meetings (virtual or face-to-face) increases the likelihood that someone would not know who his or her team leader is or who fellow team members are. Although these challenges can be daunting, in later chapters, we will discuss what the most effective virtual teams do to successfully overcome these challenges.

Four Pitfalls to Virtual Team Performance

In addition to the performance challenges virtual teams face, four pitfalls also lead to poor performance and, in some cases, to failure. Are these factors present in your organization's virtual teams?

Lack of Clear Goals, Direction, or Priorities

As with any team, virtual or co-located, a lack of clear goals and priorities will inhibit team performance. And because it is tougher to communicate with team members who are geographically distributed and keep them informed, this can be an even bigger problem for virtual teams.

For example, often, team members are not fully informed about changes in focus, which leads to a lack of clarity and frustration. One virtual team member in our study stated, "While our goals are very clear, they change so frequently, which leads to ambiguity." The most effective virtual teams reassess goals as priorities shift over time. Teams that do this effectively are usually those with the best leaders. Virtual team leaders are primarily responsible for ensuring goal clarity, resolving conflicting priorities, and ensuring the team is aware of any changes.

When new virtual teams are formed, the most effective teams outline team goals and objectives immediately. Consider two different scenarios: A global engineering team conducted a kick-off meeting to build relationships and outline team goals and responsibilities. During the meeting, the team leader clarified team member roles and established how the team would work together. Once things were underway, the leader used virtual meetings and regularly updated postings on the team's intranet site to inform team members about any updates and changes over time.

However, in our second scenario, a virtual cross-functional task force from a global investment management company experienced numerous problems with setting expectations and often failed to meet its commitments. One of the virtual team members stated, "People have no idea what our real goals are, as no one has been very clear about this from the start." The team was eventually disbanded because it had not achieved its objectives. Ironically, the team never knew what they supposed to be or do.

Lack of Clear Roles Among Team Members

In virtual teams, it is especially important for team members to clearly understand their individual roles, specifically who they report to and who reports to them. A poorly designed accountabilities structure can have a huge impact on virtual teams.

For example, if a global product development team is working virtually, it would not be efficient for team members in Asia to have to wait to check on how to proceed on a given initiative with team members in New York, who start their business day much later. What would work best is if the team members in Asia have the authority to make decisions based on their own scope of work. Designing an effective accountabilities structure minimizes delays and inefficiencies that are common when working virtually.

Given the complexity of some initiatives, role clarity is particularly important in cross-functional virtual teams. High-performing virtual teams establish clear roles up-front and continually reassess and ensure clarity of roles over time.

One global information technology team developed a great way to communicate team member roles. They created a "team handbook," which provided background on each team member and clearly laid out how each person was to contribute to the team. When questions arose during large, complex projects, team members would consult the handbook to determine which team member to consult with. Many of the less-effective teams in our study did not clarify roles during their launch and often failed to revisit roles as things changed during their projects.

Lack of Cooperation

When a diverse group of individuals is asked to work together to accomplish shared objectives, it takes time to build an atmosphere of collaboration. And because there is a lack of face-to-face contact inherent in virtual teamwork, the process of developing trust and building relationships can be even more arduous.

Conflicts often arise between team members or among factions or cliques. It happens with co-located teams as well and is especially common in large teams where "subgroups" develop. For example, consider a virtual team we worked with that we will call "TeamInnovate." Two-thirds of the team's members were located in Philadelphia, and the remaining one-third were scattered in different sites around the world. Naturally, the team members in Philadelphia developed stronger relationships with one another than they did with the members who worked outside the main "hub."

Unfortunately, this setup led to the formation of subgroups, which began to impede team collaboration. Several team members routinely worked together on projects and didn't keep other team members informed, which, over time, led to a lack of trust among team members.

Differences of opinion can also hinder collaboration. The high-performing virtual teams in our study were able to handle conflict better than the low-performing teams. In many situations, team members are simply not equipped with the skills necessary for effectively dealing with conflict, especially when conflicts cannot be resolved through face-to-face interaction.

A finance team in a global manufacturing company experienced this very challenge first-hand. Two separate factions developed due to different team members working closely together in each of two locations. However, team members in one location didn't collaborate with team members in the other location, which created conflict. In this particular case, team members who were co-located began having their own meetings, and they didn't include the members in the other location. Eventually, team members began to blame one another for the team's shortcomings, which, of course, only led to more conflict. Until this problem was addressed with the entire team, the team did not fully meet its objectives and many team members were dissatisfied.

A Lack of Engagement

Many virtual team members in our study reported a lack of engagement that resulted from not feeling challenged, lacking role clarity, having ineffective team leaders, and lacking meaningful goals.

A lack of engagement is not uncommon among virtual team members because it can be difficult to assess other team members' levels of engagement because they are in different locations and rarely have face-to-face interactions. To avoid this common problem, leaders and team members should proactively look for signs of disengagement.

For example, here are a few assessment questions to ask yourself: *Are all team members contributing to conversations and projects? Are they attending and actively participating in team meetings? Are team members motivated to take on new work or are they feeling overwhelmed? Are people working well together or is there frequent and unproductive team conflict?*

Looking out for these common red flags can help prevent engagement issues from derailing a team.

Let's take another look at "TeamInnovate." Several of the team's members reported feelings of isolation and a lack of connectivity with others on the team. In a virtual setting, this is very common. People easily become bored and "check out" because there is a lack of dynamic face-to-face interaction and because there are more distractions.

One virtual team member expressed frustration with her team, which was not performing effectively: "We are all so used to nonproductive meetings so we typically just mute our phones and don't really pay attention, which isn't effective." So if you are a virtual team leader, be constantly assessing your team members' levels of engagement. If you monitor your virtual team's performance to ensure that the team is always fully engaged, the team's effectiveness will be much improved.

Conclusion

Given the prevalence of virtual teamwork and its importance in achieving business objectives, we were surprised by how many teams are ineffective. But what was most startling is that many companies either do not realize that their virtual teams are underperforming or, despite their investments in these teams, they do not take the time to focus on enhancing their effectiveness. The good news is that there are numerous strategies that organizations and team leaders can employ that will improve the performance of their virtual teams.

The Bottom Line

Organizations that proactively take steps to support virtual teams as well as periodically assess their effectiveness will see a much better ROI than organizations that are complacent.

Chapter Two

Profiles of Virtual Team Success—What Good Looks Like

"Excellence is a better teacher than mediocrity.
The lessons of the ordinary are everywhere. Truly
profound and original insights are to be found only
in studying the exemplary."

—*Warren G. Bennis*

As Warren Bennis suggests in the quote that kicks off this chapter, there are numerous benefits associated with "studying the exemplary." We at OnPoint believe that, too. And so do our clients—we are frequently asked to describe how top-performing virtual teams benchmark effectiveness.

We're regularly asked, *What team size is optimal? Do cross-functional teams have more challenges? How often should virtual teams meet face-to-face?* These and similar questions led to our research study, in which we collected data to better understand high-performing virtual teams so that we could provide practical research-based recommendations to leaders and managers.

As part of our study, we profiled top-performing virtual teams and found that the characteristics that emerged fell into three categories: team composition, communication and training, and leadership. Let's explore each one.

Team Composition

We found that decisions about team size and membership are critical to the success of virtual teams—especially when team composition is likely to become more dynamic over time. Let's take a look at how team composition can impact performance.

Stable Team Membership

The top-performing teams in our study typically had a core group of individuals whose membership did not fluctuate frequently. On the less-effective teams, however, members were frequently added and removed. For example, one of the less-effective virtual teams we spoke with indicated that their membership changed on a monthly basis. This caused confusion about who was on the team and also led to role ambiguity. With less frequent changes in membership, the high-performing teams we studied had greater stability and more time for members to build productive work relationships.

We also found that less-effective virtual teams had difficulty accurately reporting team size, perhaps because the numbers changed so frequently. One team we interviewed was actually made up of twelve members, yet some of the team's members reported five while others said twenty.

Fewer Team Members

The less-effective teams in our study were also disproportionately larger. For example, 37 percent of low-performing teams had thirteen or more members, compared with just 24 percent of the top-performing teams. The bottom line is that, when geographically distributed teams become too large, it is more difficult for their members to communicate and collaborate effectively, which makes achieving collective goals a tall task.

Let's take a look at a high-performing virtual team that effectively managed team membership. Team SolveIT is a global information technology team with ten members—each in a different location. From past experience, the head of the business unit at SolveIT's organization learned that smaller, cohesive teams are more effective. (The organization had previously formed larger teams so that employees would not be left out even if they did not have a clear role. Some of these team members never even participated in meetings or on projects.)

To avoid creating a team that was too large to be effective, the leader decided to keep the core team small size, but also formed advisory groups, who acted as collaborators beyond SolveIT's core members. This strategy proved to be beneficial in a number of ways. It provided the team with additional resources and brainpower when they were needed. It kept people engaged and focused. And it allowed everyone to have a clear role on the team. As a result, members of the extended team reported that the arrangement was more efficient for everyone.

Now let's contrast Team SolveIt with a team that was essentially too big to succeed. "Team FAIL," as we'll call it, is a global R&D team with eighteen team members. And while the size of the team was not the cause of all its problems, it certainly had a significant, negative impact.

Team members regularly reported a lack of trust because people did not share information with one another. They further indicated that there was ambiguity about what role each member should be playing. Also, they mentioned a lack of accountability—a few team members were doing the majority of the work while others failed to attend key meetings. And finally, when asked what they believed the performance barrier was, the majority of members pointed to the team's large size.

Team Members Are from the Same Function

Most of the high-performing teams in our study were not cross-functional, while the majority of lower-performing teams were. In a virtual environment, the complexities that come with being a cross-functional team can easily affect performance. Cross-functional teams are frequently composed of team members from different functions brought together to solve business challenges. For example, people from IT, finance, HR, and operations may work together on a cost-management initiative.

However, we found cross-functional teams to be especially susceptible to problems caused by lack of accountability. These teams operate in a matrix structure where team leaders may not have formal authority over all the members of a given team. As a result, it is more difficult for a leader to hold people accountable for their work, especially if that leader isn't effective at building commitment and influencing others.

And in the case of many of the poorly performing cross-functional teams, team members are not even evaluated based on their contributions to the team, a reality that can impede performance. In addition, less-effective virtual team leaders often do not monitor the work of cross-functional team members and, in fact, many of them haven't even implemented the necessary processes to do so.

Team Members Belong to Fewer Teams

Forty-two percent of members of low-performing teams reported that a key challenge for them was finding the time to participate on a given team because they were spread so thinly across multiple teams. However, high-performing teams did not report this as a challenge. Only 18 percent of team members on high-performing teams were on four or more virtual teams, compared to 30 percent of team members on low-performing teams.

During our interviews with members of the low-performing teams, we learned that people are frequently invited to participate on a team even if they will not have a specific role on that team. Surprisingly, this was often done so that team members did not feel left out or to avoid conflict within a department or function.

In many situations, team membership is outside of the normal job requirements. For example, people may be invited to join special task forces to investigate a customer problem or to provide recommendations. Yet, this extra work is not necessarily part of their day-to-day responsibilities. As a result, when people end up on too many virtual teams, because of time constraints they cannot fulfill all of their day-to-day obligations as well as meet all of their team deadlines.

The frequency with which this phenomenon occurs with virtual teams may be attributed to globalization and improvements in technology. Today, organizations can more easily involve local employees who are close to the problem while also leveraging the best talent available outside of the HQ.

Longer Tenure as a Team

Teams with more than three years' tenure performed better than those with less than three years' tenure. In our discussions with long-tenured teams, we learned that by working together over time they were able to successfully implement processes that support teamwork and communication. For example, experienced R&D or investment teams that had been working together for several years with very few changes to team membership had established norms and unique team practices that led to their success over time.

The winning factor here is experience. Virtual teams that have already been working together for three years know one another's strengths and weaknesses. They know who is good at solving certain problems, and they've figured out how to manage conflict and coordinate the work. Just as a co-located staff that has been together for years is likely to perform better than a staff that is just coming together, the same is true for virtual teams. The key for virtual teams that are just starting out is to look to more experienced teams to see what best practices they use. When there is an example to follow, it becomes much easier to get off to a good start.

Communication and Training

Although technology is the foundation that enables effective virtual collaboration, it doesn't guarantee successful virtual teams. Success requires using that technology to communicate effectively (and, preferably, to communicate *without* technology at times).

Face-to-Face Meetings

Our study found that virtual teams that held an initial face-to-face meeting within the first ninety days of the team coming together performed better than those who never met face-to-face. Bottom line: Face-to-face meetings may be an investment, but they're an investment that pays off.

Bringing team members together to clarify goals and roles and to get to know one another can be extremely beneficial. Yet, for various reasons, it's not always possible to hold an in-person kick-off meeting. It may not be worth the time and cost to arrange a face-to-face kick-off meeting if the virtual team has been assembled to deal with a short-term problem and will soon disband. In such instances we recommend having a series of videoconferences or web-based meetings to accomplish the same objectives.

In addition, teams that periodically met face-to-face performed significantly better than those who never met in-person. And while it's true that virtual teams can find ways to make up for the lack of face-to-face interaction, in-person meetings do seem to enhance team performance.

Effective "V-Meetings"

Sixty-three percent of higher-performing virtual teams met virtually at least once a week compared to 29 percent of the less-effective teams. Teams that met virtually (which we refer to as "v-meetings") each week were rated as the most effective.

But keep in mind that your virtual teams shouldn't be meeting—whether virtually or in person—just so they can say they did. It is better to have a small number of effective meetings than to have a bunch of ineffective ones.

Let's take a look at two examples.

A global operations team would meet via teleconference on a weekly basis. The team had a formal leader, but would rotate the role of meeting facilitator each week. The assigned facilitator was responsible for sending out a draft agenda in advance of the one-hour call to solicit team member input to help prioritize and add other agenda items. After receiving team member feedback, the facilitator would then update and redistribute the agenda. The team also rotated the role of "recorder," the member who would take "v-notes" on key action items and accountabilities.

The team always used the meeting time efficiently. They spent a few minutes providing updates and spent the majority of the rest of the time discussing ideas and reaching agreement on key decisions. Because the meetings would run so smoothly, people were engaged in the discussions and everyone offered ideas. One team member had this to say: "Our virtual meetings are highly efficient since we manage our time well. For example, we don't waste a ton of time providing basic updates to one another, as we can do this via email." After the meeting, the recorder would distribute a brief summary that outlined next steps and accountabilities.

In contrast, a global technology team in an investment management company would meet weekly via one-hour teleconferences. In this case, the team leader led each meeting and did not solicit input from team members regarding agenda items in advance of the meeting. Instead, at the beginning of each meeting, everyone on the call would spend at least fifteen minutes crafting the agenda.

And in many meetings, people provided basic updates, which often did not change significantly week-to-week. As a result, many team members did not pay attention during the calls. (I think we can almost all relate. How often have you found yourself on a conference call barely listening to what is being discussed as you read or answer emails or send instant messages?)

The leader was also responsible for recording the meeting notes, which would result in numerous delays as he would pause to write certain points. Clearly, this team would have benefited from better v-meeting management, which we discuss in detail in Chapter Seven.

Well-Leveraged Technology

Members of high-performing teams were more likely to report that they had technology that helped them work together more effectively. They also used video conferencing slightly more often than their poorly performing counterparts.

There were a few other interesting findings about the role technology plays in virtual team performance. For example, low-performing teams are more likely to suffer from technology overload or using too many different technologies, which leads to communication problems and hinders performance. In addition, they are less likely to match the technology to the task. For example, many high-performing teams use webinars and collaborative technologies for brainstorming and decision making, while low-performing teams rely more heavily on email. In some cases, low-performing teams also reported experiencing more technology problems and frequently indicated that they lacked appropriate technical training.

And perhaps most importantly, through our study we found that technology should be viewed as a catalyst for virtual team performance improvement not as an automatic remedy. In other words, simply using the technology just because you have it will not immediately solve your virtual team performance problems. You have to know how to use the right mix of technologies for your specific team.

Skill Development

Our research results indicate that virtual teams that had more than four team-development sessions performed significantly better than those that had one or fewer sessions.

Forty-five percent of those in the study said that the top skill-development needs for those working in virtual teams are communication and interpersonal skills. After that, teams selected collaboration skills, action planning, problem solving, and decision making. Twenty-seven percent also said that the ability to manage change is important, and 26 percent chose the ability to manage accountability.

When we looked to see whether the skill-development needs varied between high- and low-performing teams, there were several interesting findings. Both highly effective and moderately effective teams selected communication and interpersonal skills as their top development needs, while low-performing teams did not. However, low-performing teams reported both decision making and managing accountability as key development needs, while very few high-performing teams said the same.

Because communication is the primary hurdle virtual teams face, it was surprising to find that low-performing teams usually place little emphasis on it. There could be several reasons for this. One might be that they have more serious performance issues, such as not being able to make decisions effectively or not being able to hold one another accountable for results. But most likely, they are not performing because they do not recognize how important communication is to virtual team success.

Perhaps you're thinking, *My organization's virtual teams will never perform poorly because we have great employees.* Well, congratulations on having great employees, but unfortunately, performance issues aren't always in the team's hands. In fact, if you're a leader at your organization you might be at fault.

We found that many organizations launch virtual teams without providing the necessary training to support them. Let's say a virtual team comes together for the first time on a project, but they aren't trained properly in how to communicate and collaborate with one another. Deficiencies in those skills can snowball in a virtual setting where team members need to adapt their style and approach in order to remain productive and engaged.

And if you're putting people on virtual teams who already have performance issues and you aren't providing them with proper training, the team is pretty much doomed from the beginning. For example, people who struggle to effectively provide updates in a concise and timely manner will have even greater difficulties in these areas when collaborating from a distance.

You must carefully assess employees you are considering for virtual teams, make sure you select only those who have the appropriate skill set, and then ensure that those selected have the necessary training to be successful.

We recommend collecting data to assess the areas that are barriers for the team before providing generic training. Targeted training is more effective and is more likely to provide a better return on investment for the organization.

Remember, the most effective training sessions engage team members rather than just deliver information, and they also provide opportunities to test skills. When face-to-face training is not possible, we recommend conducting a series of brief virtual training sessions that focus on specific topics.

Know what kind of training will be effective for your specific team. All training is not creating equal. During our interviews, we heard stories about teams being asked to participate in online self-directed learning that turned out to be very long, dull, and basic. In other situations, team members talked about participating in full-day virtual training sessions that failed to provide them with any engaging activities.

Having the teams work on assignments in between sessions helps create momentum and continuity, as this provides opportunities for teams to collaborate on real-world business issues, which helps reinforce the insights and skills taught in training sessions.

Leadership

Not surprisingly, leadership plays a major role in virtual team performance. Many of the low-performing teams in our study had ineffective leaders who struggled to build collaboration within their teams, which contributed to their poor performance. And although leaders of high-performing teams faced many challenges of their own—such as a lack of resources and a lack of time to focus on leading—they handled them more effectively.

Top-performing leaders are better able to balance the people-oriented and execution-oriented responsibilities associated with managing virtual teams. (We explore the differentiators of highly effective virtual team leaders in more detail in Chapter Five.)

In Chapter One, we discussed two important pitfalls for virtual teams—the lack of clear roles and the lack of shared goals. Another pitfall should be added to that list: lack of a clear accountability structure.

We have witnessed numerous situations in which a team member might have a dotted-line reporting relationship to a team leader, when she is actually accountable to a different manager who, in many cases, has a different perspective of the team's role. When this happens, team members are pulled in different directions—which will inevitably have a negative impact on the team.

Forming teams on which members report directly to the team leader is the best way to solve this problem. Many of the leaders of the high-performing virtual teams in our study had their team members report directly to them. Doing so facilitates communication, increases the likelihood that team members have shared goals and clear roles, and enhances the leaders' ability to follow through and hold people accountable.

Some virtual team leaders find it difficult to hold people accountable, and this is a task that becomes even more of a challenge in cross-functional teams, where the leader does not have direct authority over team members.

Conclusion

We can gain many valuable insights from studying the most effective virtual teams. The methods used by the high-performing teams we've discussed here should be taken into account when forming or reorganizing virtual teams. In most cases, companies can and should control factors such as team size and skills development for virtual team members. If organizations want their virtual teams to be best-in-class, it is important that they understand what factors must come together to create that distinction—and to implement them up-front.

The Bottom Line

Paying attention to factors like communication and training, team composition, and team leadership directly impacts virtual team success.

Chapter Three

Virtual Team Launch Kit

"A lot of organizations create virtual teams with almost no understanding of the unique implications of that decision."

—Margaret A. Neale, professor,
Stanford Graduate School of Business[1]

Each year an increasing number of organizations are launching new teams whose members must collaborate and work together from a distance. While many of these teams are successful, others never accomplish their objectives. Why? Because some organizations that decide to use virtual teams do not invest the resources necessary to ensure their productivity and survival.

As a result, we frequently hear stories about missed deadlines, unhappy customers, failed product launches, and other serious costs (both monetary and non-monetary) associated with failed or failing virtual teams.

Why are some organizations and virtual teams more successful than others? The answer is actually quite simple: Organizations with high-performing virtual teams understand that those teams are unique—and thus take the appropriate actions to help them to be successful.

Test Your Virtual Team Launch IQ

Before we discuss the guidelines for effectively launching new virtual teams, let's assess your current knowledge. The case study below outlines a situation related to launching a new virtual team. We invite you to read the case study and think about how you would handle it.

Take notes about what you would do in each situation. After you've done so, use the scoring guidelines to evaluate how you did. And once you finish the chapter, consider revisiting the case study to determine what you might do differently.

Case Study: Pharmacorp

Pharmacorp is a global research-driven pharmaceutical organization that is committed to science and innovation. Its 45,000 employees are geographically dispersed around the world, with business operations in 120 countries. The majority of its products are in the immunology and cardiovascular space, but the company has recently decided to make a significant R&D investment in oncology products. Peter Frank, the company's global head of R&D, recently announced that the company would be creating a new global organizational structure for R&D that will better optimize resources to support each of its product lines.

In his announcement, Peter said that one critical component of this initiative will be launching a global task force that would examine the various alternatives to this new organizational structure and that he would be making a recommendation to the Pharmacorp senior team within the next six weeks. The task force is made up of fifteen employees within the R&D organization, who are geographically dispersed around the world. It is made clear that members of the task force will need to dedicate a significant amount of their time to it, while also continuing to focus on their day-to-day responsibilities.

Peter has requested that you lead the task force, as he feels that it will be a good developmental experience for you. Given how important it is that this task force succeed, Peter wants to meet with you tomorrow to discuss how you plan to approach this important role. In order to facilitate your discussion, he has asked that you begin outlining your approach for successfully launching and leading this team. Peter envisions having nominal financial support for this task force and suggests that you minimize team travel and expenses as much as possible.

How will you approach this challenge? What role will each team member play? How will you engage team members to ensure their commitment? Take some time to write down your ideas and approach. After you do, review the factors below and check the ones you considered as you thought about how you would approach the situation.

❑ Consider the objective and work of the task force and determine whether there are clear roles for each of the fifteen members. If there are not, initiate a discussion with Peter and consider reducing the size of the team.

❑ Evaluate your own strengths and weaknesses as a virtual team leader to identify pitfalls you want to avoid as you take on this development responsibility.

❑ Schedule a face-to-face kick-off meeting to clarify the purpose and focus of the task force and begin to build relationships.

❑ Clarify how both individual and team performance will be measured and recognized.

❑ As the virtual team leader, ensure you have a clear understanding of your own role and responsibilities; share this with the team.

❑ Ask the team for their input on how to operate effectively and efficiently.

❑ Establish in the beginning how progress will be monitored and the best means for communicating progress (weekly or bi-weekly calls, when to communicate progress via the phone, email or video conferencing).

❑ Because the team members do not report directly to you and are responsible for fulfilling their day-to-day responsibilities in addition to their work on the task force, consider how people will be held accountable and how competing priorities will be handled.

Are You Ready to Launch a Virtual Team?

Next, use the guidelines in Table 3.1 to determine how effectively you evaluated the situation.

Table 3.1 Evaluating Your Responses

Number of Items Checked	Interpretation
6 to 8	You have considered the majority of the factors required to successfully launch a virtual team.
5	You have considered most of the factors required to successfully launch a virtual team.
4	You have considered some of the factors required to successfully launch a virtual team.
3	You have considered a few of the factors required to successfully launch a virtual team.

How did you do? Were you surprised by how much you already knew about preparing a virtual team for success? Or did you overlook some of the factors required for virtual success? If you missed some important factors, you'll find this chapter particularly helpful. And if you scored a 6, 7, or 8, please don't skip to the next chapter just yet. Read on to find tips and tools to help you continue to improve your process and approach.

Setting Virtual Teams Up for Success

Many organizations quickly assemble virtual teams to address emerging business challenges. For example, one global investment management company would frequently establish new virtual teams to come up with solutions to address customer complaints.

However, when doing so, company leaders often pulled people together who had never worked with one another before and did not provide the necessary resources to ensure these teams would be effective. Many of the teams lacked a clear direction, and members were often too busy to dedicate quality time to the team.

So what should this organization have done differently? We would give them the same advice we'd give anyone launching a virtual team—advice we've laid out in the "roadmap" below to help get *your* teams off to a fast, effective start.

Before the Launch: Forming a Virtual Team

When we looked at the differences between the most- and least-effective virtual teams, we found that the most effective teams thought through four key questions before they even reached the official launch stage:

1. How many people should be on the team?
2. Do the team leader and team members have the right combination of technical and "virtual" skills to work effectively in a virtual environment?
3. Will the team have access to the technology they need to effectively communicate and share information?
4. How will the team and the individual team members be recognized and rewarded?

Keep Your Virtual Teams at a Manageable Size. As we discussed, our research found that high-performing virtual teams were smaller and more cohesive than low-performing ones. For a team to make decisions effectively and operate efficiently, its ideal size should be five to eight people.

When forming a new virtual team, consider who really needs to be included and make sure each member has a clear role. As more and more people become involved, virtual teams may be more susceptible to common pitfalls such as a lack of clear roles or clear goals. If you have larger virtual teams in your organization, we recommend they be broken into sub-teams responsible for a specific deliverable or a core team with advisory groups so that they can communicate and function effectively in a virtual setting.

While it's true that team members often participate on virtual teams in addition to their day-to-day responsibilities, participation on multiple virtual teams should be limited so members can dedicate the time required to fulfill their team roles successfully. Organizations need to be thoughtful about team membership and ensure that they are not encouraging their employees to over-commit themselves.

Choose Virtual Team Leaders Carefully. The most effective virtual team leaders are able to balance both the execution-oriented practices and the interpersonal, communication, and cultural factors that define virtual teams. Therefore, organizations should select as leaders only people who possess those key characteristics.

Unfortunately, many organizations do not put as much thought as they should into their team leader decisions. In fact, we often hear stories about team leaders who were selected based on availability or simply because they volunteered. Remember, leading a virtual team is a challenging task and requires a different skill set than leading a traditional co-located team.

When assigning a leader, organizations should take the time to select the individual with the appropriate skills—and not just go with the first person to volunteer or someone who already happens to lead a team. In addition, they should periodically assess their leaders' effectiveness and provide them with targeted feedback about how they can enhance their performance. Great leaders will be happy to learn what they can do to keep improving.

Make Sure Teams Have the Right Mix of "Virtual" and Technical Skills. Organizations should also ensure that their virtual team members have the skills necessary to effectively collaborate from a distance. People who are motivated and able to work in a self-directed manner, have a tolerance for ambiguity, are strong communicators, and are collaborative will be more effective on virtual teams.

A recent *BusinessWeek* article[2] presented findings on what personality traits make for good virtual workers. While one might assume that introverted people would be more likely to thrive in a virtual setting, the study found that it was actually extroverts who fared best. It was discovered that extroverted employees were more adept at finding ways to stay connected to others, no matter their location. The study also showed that being structured and organized is essential for successfully working virtually, and that disorganized employees were less successful.

Organizations generally need to make sure team members have the appropriate skills for tackling particular tasks. Laszlo Bock of Google says, "It is important to compose the team differently based on the problem the team needs to solve or address." For example, the people chosen to help solve a detailed financial problem would most likely *not* be selected for a virtual team that's created to tackle a customer satisfaction issue.

However, in some situations organizations benefit from the use of cross-functional teams, in which they bring together people with different areas of expertise to address a problem. Bottom line: It is important to consider the scope of the problem to determine the criteria for virtual team membership.

You can start by establishing criteria for selecting team members. For example, a global IT virtual team in our study outlined the skill set necessary for success and then selected team members accordingly. While technical expertise in various IT areas was deemed important, the leader wanted to involve people who would work well autonomously yet who could also successfully collaborate with the rest of the team when needed.

According to our interviews and study data, the most important characteristics for virtual team members include strong communication and interpersonal skills, initiative, and flexibility. Consider who needs to be on your virtual teams to ensure that high-quality decisions are made and across-the-board buy-in is achieved.

Understanding the characteristics necessary for succeeding in a virtual environment is very important. While these characteristics may vary depending on a virtual team's goals, the checklist provided in Table 3.2 can be used to help organizations select virtual team members and leaders.

Table 3.2 Checklist for Virtual Team Leader
and Team Member Selection

A Good Virtual Team Leader	A Good Virtual Team Member
❑ Delegates work and responsibilities effectively; trusts others to achieve goals	❑ Demonstrates a high level of motivation
❑ Implements processes to effectively monitor work (checks in without micromanaging, has strong project management skills)	❑ Effectively communicates with others (reaches out to others for help and proactively shares information with others)
❑ Effectively manages conflict	❑ Effectively collaborates with others
❑ Is comfortable working in an unstructured environment	❑ Is comfortable working in an unstructured environment
❑ Demonstrates strong communication and management skills (provides clear direction and is responsive)	❑ Is able to operate autonomously to achieve goals/objectives
❑ Inspires people to achieve results	❑ Is self-disciplined
❑ Effectively recognizes and rewards others	❑ Is proficient with technology
❑ Provides coaching and feedback to others; supports others	❑ Efficiently uses time and resources to carry out objectives
❑ Appropriately consults and engages others when making decisions	❑ Resolves work-related problems quickly
❑ Holds others accountable for meeting commitments	❑ Takes full accountability for decisions, actions, and performance

Select the Right Communication Technologies. Even more than other members of the organization, virtual team members need a way to communicate effectively, share information, raise concerns, ask for help, obtain answers to questions, and brainstorm. It's also important for them to be able to leverage tools that help compensate for the lack of face-to-face interaction in a virtual setting.

In order for virtual collaboration to be truly successful, the right technologies must be available. There are many ways to implement effective communication such as team v-meetings, emailing, videoconferencing, instant messaging, collaborative group technologies, blogs, wikis, and web-based bulletin boards.

We find that it's best to use a mix of communication methods. For example, to help increase engagement and social interaction, some organizations have created team websites or use collaborative tools that function as "virtual water coolers" to encourage informal team communication.

Other virtual teams have created shared spaces using social networking–based tools such as Facebook to help team members get to know one another and strengthen interpersonal relationships. These tools allow team members to learn about one another despite the lack of face-to-face contact.

Access to instant messaging tools also allows team members to interact in a more immediate and spontaneous manner that is similar to how they would communicate if they were co-located. And conducting meetings via a videoconference is another great way to overcome the lack of face-to-face interaction.

The team should determine at the outset how it will communicate, and at that time members should have any necessary training needed to successfully and easily use the communication technologies. If you'd like to learn more about this, we discuss criteria for matching the technology to the task in Chapter Seven.

Determine How Performance Will Be Recognized and Rewarded. When virtual team members are consistently recognized and rewarded for their achievements, their commitment to the team and to the organization is reinforced and they stay motivated. A lack of engagement, one of the pitfalls we discussed in Chapter One, is common when virtual team members receive little recognition.

When a new virtual team is established at your organization, consider the best ways to recognize its individual members, the team as a whole, and its leader. As the team's work gets underway and progresses, make sure members are consistently recognized for their achievements. This is particularly important when people join virtual teams on a voluntary basis.

It's important that organizations and virtual team leaders develop strategies to reward and recognize virtual teams and their members. For example, find opportunities to "spotlight" team members and to virtually celebrate successes as a team. Some leaders use e-certificates, e-newsletters, and other online mechanisms to recognize team members.

It's also important to communicate successes to virtual team members' managers, as they may not be aware of their employees' achievements. Sahota at Schering-Plough explained that the company's recognition system is designed to allow team leaders to include the team members' managers on recognition emails and other communication for this very reason.

For consistency's sake, virtual team reward systems should be aligned with any existing organizational performance management systems. And traditional organizational incentives and systems may need to be adapted for use in a virtual environment. For example, recognition ceremonies that might normally be done at a face-to-face team meeting or dinner would now need to be done during a phone call or video conference. And trophies and plaques recognizing special contributions would have to be mailed after they're awarded rather than handed out at the time of the announcement.

It's also important to ensure that the reward and recognition systems promote collaboration among team members.

Consider an organization that bases virtual team members' incentives on how each person performs relative to the other members of the team (versus relative to their individual performance goals). Although this approach certainly motivates each individual to reach higher levels of productivity, it also has an unintended consequence: It does not encourage teamwork and cooperation.

Virtual team members start to think, *Why should I help my co-worker when enhancing her performance may negatively impact my level of recognition and reward?* This is a valid point. While it is beneficial to implement some system to inspire virtual team members and reward their performance, it's also important to ensure that these systems help unite rather than divide team members.

Group celebrations and bonuses shared by all team members might be effective rewards for some virtual teams. Whenever possible involve the team's senior sponsors and stakeholders in the recognition process in formal and informal ways. Doing so will help further motivate team members because they'll see that their work is appreciated from the top down.

The Launch Stage: Hold a Great Kick-Off Meeting

As we mentioned earlier, face time counts. While meeting in person requires time and costs money, our research shows that virtual teams that have an initial kick-off meeting perform better than those that do not. To facilitate team performance, we recommend that companies invest the time and money to bring members together within the first thirty days of the team's inception.

Kick-off meetings help get everyone on the same page. Virtual team members learn about the scope of the work or project, get to know the people who are on their team, and come to a consensus on team structure and processes. These sessions also allow time for members to develop a team plan and to build interpersonal relationships.

The synergies and significant long-term payoff gained from working face-to-face on setting team norms, processes, and relationship building appear to outweigh the expense of travel. Laszlo Bock agrees that in-person kick-off meetings for teams at Google are critical. He says, "The single biggest challenge is building trust. Unless you build it up-front, you start seeing politics or people disengaging, which results in negative behavior. We try to have face-to-face kick-off meetings, which completely changes the nature of the team. If you do it early on, it has a huge impact versus doing it later when you are repairing things."

An effective kick-off meeting will accomplish the following goals:

Create a Sense of Purpose. Having a sense of purpose and a clear understanding of how the virtual team contributes to the organization's overall goals helps build a sense of unity and provides direction and motivation for team members. These matters should be communicated early and often while a team is working together.

The "Purpose Pyramid"[3] in Figure 3.1 describes the four building blocks required to create a sense of purpose for your virtual team. One factor that contributes to a team feeling that it

Figure 3.1 The Purpose Pyramid

has a sense of purpose is based on team members' understanding of the organization's purpose and vision and how the team is connected to "big picture."

Although it is not realistic to expect to build a strong sense of purpose at a one- or two-day kick-off meeting, you can expect to build a solid foundation. A portion of the meeting can be focused on how the virtual team's deliverables are aligned with the organization's purpose and vision and the impact they have on customers. For example, when a global pharmaceutical R&D team understands how the drug they are developing will help patients with the disease and its work relates to the strategy of their organization (that is, why we are in this business), it clearly emphasizes the individual and team contribution in a very concrete way.

The last element that impacts sense of purpose, the quality of relationships with other members of the team, is also important to begin working on during the kick-off meeting. The majority of the agenda items should be directed toward helping team members get to know each other better, building a sense of community/team, and clarifying when collaboration is needed and what it looks like when it is. As you will see later in this chapter, a variety of experiential and real-world activities can help teams accomplish this objective.

The checklist in Exhibit 3.1 below outlines the actions that help create a sense of team purpose.

Exhibit 3.1. Monitor Your Sense of Purpose

Using the scale below, assess what you feel you currently do well and where you will need some improvement. This can also be used as a checklist to monitor and assess your ongoing efforts to create a sense of purpose.

1 = I rarely do this
2 = I do this some of the time
3 = I do this frequently

1. **The Organization**

_____ Help my virtual team have an explicitly clear understanding of our organizational purpose—as a company and as a team.

_____ Communicate a very clear vision of where we need to go in the future; give my team members something to strive for—as a company and as a team.

_____ Communicate, live by, and reinforce a distinct set of values—as a company and as a team.

2. **Relationship to the Organization**

_____ Help each member of my virtual team feel like he/she makes a difference.

_____ Encourage continuous improvement and innovation.

_____ Keep virtual team members connected to the "big picture."

3. **Self**

_____ Create a workplace in which team members can pursue their personal values.

_____ Give team members challenges that are motivating and realistic.

_____ Create, support, and reinforce employee learning and development.

_____ Ensure team members have what they need to achieve their goals.

4. **Relationship to Others**

_____ Build a sense of community within the virtual team

_____ Champion collaboration, helping others, and cooperation

_____ Keep a constant focus on the customer

_____ Seek to involve team members to create a sense of ownership

---

Clarify the Team's Goals. It's critical to discuss the team's overriding goals and plans for achieving these goals. As part of this, we also recommend discussing how the team will assess its performance and how it will establish key milestones and performance metrics. Where possible, involve team members in discussions about setting or prioritizing goals to increase their buy-in. Also, it's important to put a process in place to set and reset priorities over time.

A simple and familiar tool that will ensure the team's goal statements are unambiguous, measurable, and realistic is the SMART criteria:

- *Specific:* The goal should be expressed in terms of a specific outcome or result for which the team will be held accountable. This outcome should be linked to a specific business objective.
- *Measurable:* The goal should be expressed in terms of an outcome that can be measured or otherwise verified.
- *Aligned:* The goal should be challenging but realistic given the current environment, available resources, and the team's experience and skill level.
- *Realistic:* The goal should be consistent with the organization's/team's strategic objectives.
- *Time-bound:* The goal should include a target date or deadline by which it will be met.

Clarify Team Members' Roles. Ensure that each team member understands his or her role and responsibilities, as well as the roles of his or her fellow members. Lack of clear roles and responsibilities results in conflicts among team members or departments and can lead to situations in which key tasks fall through the cracks because no one believes they are responsible for them. This is even more prevalent in a virtual environment, where it can be more difficult to monitor others' work and hold one another accountable. Team members' level of cooperation is generally higher when everyone involved agrees on when collaboration is needed or not and what collaboration looks like in these situations. When we know what to expect from other people, we are more willing to trust them and cooperate with them.

A practical tool to help clarify roles and responsibilities, shown in Exhibit 3.2, is commonly referred to as the RACIN model, which stands for five levels of authority and involvement—Responsible, Approve, Consult, Inform, and Not Involved—and enables individuals and teams to describe what cooperation and collaboration looks like for the most important decisions and activities for which they are responsible.

During the kick-off meeting, the team starts by listing the critical decisions and activities for which they are accountable and then discusses and reaches agreement on who has which role. This takes time but is well worth the investment. Over time, most teams will eventually come to some agreement about when and how to cooperate. However, that journey can be long and arduous and frequently leads to damaged relationships and broken trust. Bottom line: Working out roles at the early stage of a virtual team's life cycle helps accelerate productivity and helps team members avoid conflict down the road.

Exhibit 3.2. The RACIN Model

Responsible

If a group or person is "responsible" for a decision or activity, then he or she is charged with "making it happen." The "R's" have the lead role in bringing all the necessary resources (people, time, funding) together to ensure that the decision or activity is carried out successfully. In many cases, an "R" is the project manager and carries out the planning; identifies who needs to be involved; communicates with other team members (that is, interfaces with the "A's," "C's," and "I's"), influences others to attain the necessary help, resources, and information; and coordinates the work.

Approve

If a group or person has the responsibility to "approve" a decision or activity, then he or she has a "go or no-go" say in carrying out the decision or activity. For example, while the "R's" may propose how to carry out the decision and how to do the work, the "A's" ultimately decide whether the plan will go forward. Therefore, the "A" in this case also stands for "accountable." The "A's" are ultimately accountable for the outcome of their decisions and the success of the work.

It's important that "R's" engage "A's" early and often in their project planning to ensure their plans are on track. Likewise, "A's" should frequently check in with "R's" to monitor progress and ensure they have the information they need to make informed approvals or disapprovals. The relationship between "R's" and "A's" should be one of constant communication and partnership.

Consult

If a person or group has this level of authority for an important decision or activity, then they should be consulted prior to making decisions. This suggests that the "C's" work is significantly affected by "R's" work and "A's" final decisions. If the "R" neglects to involve the "C" early, this can lead to a lack of "buy-in" for the critical decision or activity that the "R" is trying to implement. Typically, the "R's" should consult with the "C's" prior to asking for the "A's" approval because the "C's" input may affect how the "R's" are viewing the work/project and the primary decisions/approvals needed.

Inform

A group or person with this level of authority should be informed of the decision and other pertinent information that may affect him or her. The "R" would typically be the one to inform the "I" once the "A" has approved the final decision or plan. The information may modestly affect what the "I" is trying to accomplish, but it would not have nearly the impact that it does on the "C."

Not Involved

These groups or individuals do not need to be involved and will not be affected at all by the decision or activity.

Develop Team Norms. Clarify expectations regarding acceptable and unacceptable behaviors for team members, such as:

- Team meeting etiquette (including expectations for participating in team meetings and v-meetings)
- Expectations for collaboration, communication, and dealing with conflicts

- Process and time frame for responding to emails and telephone messages
- Review and approval process for team members' tasks

Develop a Plan for Communicating Among Team Members. Agree on the types of technology members will use to communicate and how the team's progress will be shared with stakeholders and management figures. Be sure to:

- Illustrate the connection between team activities and technological infrastructure
- Clarify communication needs and desires of team members
- Identify when face-to-face meetings should be used
- Train team members on communication technologies

During the kick-off meeting, new virtual teams will benefit from discussing how and when team members will use the available technologies. For example, how will the team share documents and update one another? Is email the best tool for this or is there another preferred mechanism?

What communication technology will be best for conflict resolution? How about for brainstorming solutions to problems? What decisions are best for teleconferences or other collaborative e-tools?

Are any key technologies not available for the team? Will this lack of availability create problems for the team? If so, what accommodations need to be made and how will the team minimize the impact?

The Virtual Team Technology Assessment in Table 3.3 is a resource to help new virtual teams think through their use of different technologies.

Hold Team Development Activities. Virtual team members often have a hard time establishing trust with one another because they don't have the advantage of frequent in-person interactions. They also struggle because they cannot see one another's body language, which makes it difficult to gain a sense for team members' personalities and intentions.

Table 3.3 Virtual Team Technology Assessment

Technology	When/How the Team Will Use It
Videoconferencing/TelePresence	
Collaborative Groupware/ Web-Based Tools	
Telephone Conferencing	
Team Website (e.g., on intranet)	
Email	
Instant Messaging	
Blogs/Wikis	
Other	

We highly recommend using team development activities during the kick-off meeting to build trust and camaraderie among team members. Many of the most successful teams in the study had skill-development training during their initial kick-off meeting and subsequent training over time.

In our work with virtual teams, we found that three activities during the launch meeting help team members get to know each other, build confidence in each other's ability, and provide a platform for teamwork and communication back on the job. They are (1) personal introductions including background and experience, (2) review of individual style and how it affects teamwork and communication, and (3) an experiential exercise or team project.

Get to Know Each Other. It wouldn't be unusual for a group of people who do not know each other very well to have pre-conceived notions about one another or to make assumptions about one another based on stereotypes or something they've heard from a third party. A great way to dispel incorrect assumptions and help team members build relationships is an icebreaker exercise that gives team members a chance to learn more about each other.

For example, ask team members to meet in pairs and ask one another the following questions: *What is your work and educational experience? Describe your greatest accomplishments at work and any special projects in which you've participated. What articles, papers, and/or books have you published? Do you have any patents? What are your hobbies and interests?*

After that, have one member of the pair introduce the other person and then continue the process until everyone has a turn. Exercises like this one can be a fun way to build relationships and engage people.

Clarify Your Team Player Style. In order to enhance collaboration, many virtual teams benefit from understanding the styles of other team members. Self-assessment questionnaires are great tools teams can use to evaluate their individual and collective work styles.

For example, Parker's[4] *Team Player Style* self-assessment helps team members increase their individual effectiveness, assess team dynamics, and understand one another's contribution to team effectiveness. Exhibit 3.3 provides a high level description of Parker's four styles. The results from the self-assessment help team members understand the advantages and potential downsides of each style and what they need to do to enhance team performance.

Exhibit 3.3. Parker's Team Player Styles

The Contributor

Task-oriented, data provider. Pushes the team to make efficient, effective progress. Wants the team to stay on track. Shares openly, delivers on his or her promises and expects others to do the same.

The Collaborator

Very goal-directed and a "big-picture" thinker. Willing to move outside of his or her defined role if it helps the team to achieve its goals. Pitches in—offers help and is relatively flexible.

The Communicator

Process-oriented, highly effective listener and facilitator of total participation. Good problem "namer" and solver, this role focuses a lot of energy on the quality of team relationships.

The Challenger

Critique-oriented, openly questioning goals, methods, or even the results. Highly ethical and willing to take risks, this role pushes the team to think from different or diverse perspectives.

Adapted from Parker, 1996.

Do Something Together. Giving the group a project to complete while they are together at the kick-off meeting is a very effective way to promote teamwork and to give people a chance to get to know each other better. The project can be either an experiential team-problem-solving exercise or based on a problem the team is actually facing.

The experiential exercise usually challenges the team to either build something (like a tower or a space module) or to solve a problem (such as surviving in the desert or developing a new product for a fictitious company). In either case they must work together to successfully accomplish their objective. As a result, team members better understand each other's work styles, preferences, and values.

Using a real-world team issue or problem accomplishes the same objective with, of course, the additional advantage of getting real work done. As the team works together to tackle these problems, the members begin to see and believe in each other's abilities.

While these steps represent an up-front investment of time and resources, the efforts pay off. Mark Gasta of Vail Resorts asserts, "It goes back to making an early investment to get people aligned from the start. It is critically important to build trust, establish norms, and clarify roles. Too often, you run the risk of these things becoming disconnected. It is inherently more difficult to apply these practices in virtual teams, but the end product is much more successful."

After the initial kick-off meeting, distribute agreements and outline any agreed-on next steps. And remember that, while these steps will set your virtual teams up for success, many challenges will emerge as team members get to know one another and begin to work together. That's why it's also important to continuously monitor team progress.

After the Launch: Monitor and Assess Team Performance

Organizations need to have a system in place that helps them regularly review virtual team processes to assess what's working well and what needs to be improved. For example, organizations should consider how effectively their teams are collaborating, making decisions, and solving problems.

Organizations should also continually monitor, assess, and improve communication, as it's the top skill-development need reported by team members and the top characteristic needed to lead from a distance.

And most importantly, they must periodically examine how well the team is performing. Performance levels can be assessed by collecting feedback from various stakeholders through online surveys such as the one used in our global study or through periodic interviews to discuss the team's effectiveness.

It's evident from our study findings and our consulting work that many organizations are surprised to find that their virtual teams are not fully performing. That's why it's critical to have processes in place to identify barriers to high performance and steps that can be taken to overcome them.

Is Your Organization Prepared to Support Virtual Team Work?

Although preparation before the launch and a well-designed face-to-face kick-off meeting are essential to virtual team success, they won't have the expected payoff if the overall organization isn't prepared to support virtual teamwork. Organizations that proactively plan how to best structure their virtual teams and take steps to set them up for success will see a better return on their investment than those that do not. Exhibit 3.4 provides an organizational checklist that outlines the key factors necessary for virtual teamwork.

Exhibit 3.4. Checklist for Virtual Teamwork

√ **Systems and Processes**
- ❏ Our technology supports virtual teamwork.
- ❏ We have adequate resources to support virtual teams.
- ❏ Our performance management system is set up to measure team and individual team member performance.
- ❏ We have reward/recognition systems that can be used for virtual teams.
- ❏ We have systems and metrics to assess virtual team/leader performance.

√ **People**
- ❏ Team leaders and team members have the skills necessary to work from a distance.
- ❏ We have practices in place that help us select virtual team leaders and members based on the situation.
- ❏ We have skills-based training for virtual teams.
- ❏ We have technology-based training for virtual teams.
- ❏ Senior leaders support virtual teamwork.

Conclusion

The most effective teams think through four key questions before they even reach the official launch stage: *How many people should be on the team? Do the team leader and the team members have the right combination of technical skills and the skills to work effectively in a virtual environment? Will the team have access to the technology they need to effectively communicate and share information? How will the team and the individual team members be recognized and rewarded?*

They also invest the time and resources to ensure their virtual teams get off to a good start. That often means holding a kick-off meeting during which they seek to achieve the following goals:

- Create a sense of purpose
- Clarify the team's goals
- Clarify team members' roles
- Develop team norms
- Develop a plan for communicating among team members
- Hold team development activities

All this work, however, will not have the intended effect if the entire organization isn't able to create and maintain an environment and systems that support virtual team work.

The Bottom Line

The decision to launch a virtual team should not be made on a whim. Factors such as team membership, team size, the right technology, and effective kick-off meetings should be carefully considered before launching a virtual team. It is also important to ensure the overall organization is prepared to support virtual team work.

Chapter Four

What Differentiates Great Virtual Teams—How to RAMP Up Your Team's Performance

"Globally linked virtual teams will transform every government and company in the world. Any of our peers who don't do it won't survive."

—*John Chambers, CEO, Cisco*[1]

What Differentiates Top Virtual Teams?

If you've spent any time looking for information about virtual teams, it's likely you haven't come up empty-handed. Still, while there are numerous articles presenting tips and best practices for virtual teams, there's little information out there on what makes top-performing virtual teams so successful. For example, you probably won't find much information on what practices differentiate high-performing virtual teams from those that are less effective.

The dearth of information on this topic led OnPoint to conduct a global research study. As part of our research, which included forty-eight virtual teams of varying levels of effectiveness, we identified five practices and characteristics that differentiate the highest and lowest performing virtual teams. These differentiators—commitment and engagement, shared processes for decision making, information flow, trust, and collaboration—are the most important components of optimal virtual team performance.

Differentiator 1: Commitment and Engagement

In our study, we found that members of high-performing virtual teams are more proactive and engaged and also demonstrate higher levels of initiative. When assessed on the item, "This team demonstrates a high level of initiative," high-performing teams in our study received an average score of 3.60 (on a 4-point scale where 1 = strongly disagree and 4 = strongly agree) versus an average of 3.06 received by low-performing teams.

The low-performing teams' poor score isn't necessarily surprising. People are often on numerous teams in addition to their day-to-day work, and it can be challenging to manage all the competing demands. However, it seems those on top-performing virtual teams are more motivated to go "above and beyond"—to do more that what's required to achieve team success.

Team leaders also play a role in commitment and engagement. Effective leaders inspire their teams and have processes in place that help them regularly monitor members' motivation levels. This leadership practice is especially important when teams work together over a long period of time, as members can become disengaged and may lose interest.

Even though the majority of virtual teams had someone assigned as the team leader, members on the high-performing teams proactively took on leadership responsibilities while members on less-effective teams were less likely to do so. Specifically, team members on high-performing teams took on additional responsibilities to reduce the burden of the official team leader.

It's important that virtual team members be willing and able to share the "leader" role. It makes sense that the role of a formal leader may be less pronounced on a virtual team (if members weren't able to perform with little direction they wouldn't be effective working virtually in the first place). Moreover, leading or participating on these teams is often outside the scope of peoples' day-to-day jobs, which means competing responsibilities often pull them away. Because of this, team members must be ready and willing to "fill the gap" and step up to the leadership plate when needed.

High-performing virtual teams also understand how their work aligns with the strategy of their organization. Our study found that, when asked how clear they were about how the team's work contributed to organizational success, high-performing teams had an average score of 3.45, while low-performing teams scored an average of 2.93.

Virtual teams that connect their day-to-day work to the organization's business strategy and objectives are more likely to stay committed and engaged over time. (Remember, disengagement can be a big problem for people working virtually.) Effective team leaders reinforce this connection by periodically reminding team members of the importance of their work and clarifying how it contributes to the success of the organization.

Differentiator 2: Shared Processes for Decision Making

We also found that high-performing virtual teams did a better job at establishing decision-making and problem-solving processes than low-performing ones. The average rating for high-performing teams on "Has a shared process for decision making/problem solving," was 3.33, while the average for low-performing teams was only 2.72. Moreover, low-performing teams had an average score of 2.86 on decision involvement, whereas top performing teams had an average of 3.14.

Ensuring that the appropriate people get the right information and are involved in important decisions can be especially challenging for virtual teams, whose members are often in different time zones and/or whose conversations are conducted primarily over the phone or via email. To help alleviate this challenge, effective virtual team leaders ensure that communication processes are established early on and revisit them over time. For example, many of the top-performing teams in our study took time soon after forming to discuss how they were going to make decisions and solve problems.

Differentiator 3: Getting the Right Information to the Right People

It's easy to see why virtual teams face significant communication challenges. Most must operate with little face-to-face contact between members and/or must work around time zone differences. And these problems can be exacerbated when cross-cultural differences exist.

High-performing virtual teams find ways to overcome these communication challenges, while their low-performing counterparts are rarely able to. In our study, high-performing teams received an average rating of 3.29 on the Communication dimension compared to an average of 2.82 for low-performing teams (which means that members of high-performing virtual teams tend to respond quickly when problems arise, provide each other with information needed to do the job, involve each other in decisions, and provide each other with feedback).

Members of low-performing teams seemed to work autonomously, often duplicating work and failing to communicate or provide feedback to one another. These teams scored an average of 2.56 on receiving the necessary feedback to do their jobs and an average of 2.80 on providing timely feedback to one another. Conversely, high-performing virtual teams scored 3.15 and 3.28, respectively, in these areas, which indicates they do a much better job communicating and sharing information.

Top-performing virtual teams also better leverage various technologies for communicating with and providing updates to one another. They rated the item "Has determined the most appropriate ways to communicate" an average of 3.27, compared to the average rating of 2.72 the low-performing teams gave.

One very successful global product development teams in our study created an effective communication strategy. They had weekly teleconferences where everyone came together to brainstorm and share ideas. In between meetings, team members communicated by email, instant messaging, the team's intranet, telephone, and webinars.

When asked what made the team so successful, one member stated, "There is very good knowledge transfer and cooperation among team members. Everyone shares information and works together. This is one of the best teams I have worked on."

On the other hand, a member of a less-effective team (in a different organization) reported that "We often don't have the necessary information to do our work. There needs to be a way for people to respond to one another and provide feedback, as there really isn't a way for people to communicate as a team collectively." These different perspectives highlight the importance of creating an effective team communication strategy.

Differentiator 4: Task-Based Trust

In his *Academy of Management Executive* article on working virtually, Wayne Cascio[2] emphasized the importance of trust for virtual teams. He wrote, "Lack of trust can undermine every other precaution taken to ensure successful virtual work arrangements."

Trust is key for virtual team success because members rarely see one another and, quite often, have never met in person. Co-located teams rely on interpersonal trust, which is based on personal relationships. Virtual teams must rely on task-based trust, which is the belief that team members will do their jobs.

Of course, task-based trust doesn't happen on its own. It has to be created—and that occurs when virtual team members are responsive, follow through on commitments, and take responsibility for results. As Swroop Sahota, vice president of Global Quality Services at Schering-Plough, observes, "The simplest way to build trust is to honor your word by meeting your objectives and responsibilities. When I do this, team members know that they can trust me. Trust is a big concept, so it is important to start with small steps."

Our study found that top-performing virtual teams have significantly higher levels of task-based trust than low-performing teams. Specifically, these top performers had an average score of 3.52 on the item "Team members trust one another to get things done," while the average for low-performing teams was 3.12.

Regarding the lack of trust we found, a team member on a low-performing team said, "People do not seem to trust one another for some reason. I am not really sure why, but it is clear that we have a problem here."

When we looked at some characteristics of that respondent's team, we found it suffered from silos, lack of communication, lack of efficient decision-making processes, and lack of transparency. We also found that team members micromanaged one another and there was duplication of work—both of which impeded productivity and led to frustration.

One member of an ineffective virtual team said, "People do not always know what skills other people have, which leads to mistrust. Then, people do not fully hand things off to one another."

In contrast, when members of a New York Life virtual team, one of the top-performing teams in our study, were asked in one-on-one interviews what could be done to improve trust, they unanimously responded that there was already a high level of trust among team members. For example, one team member stated, "We all trust one another to get things done and meet our shared goals, which makes our team very effective."

Virtual teams that are successful ensure that team members build relationships and learn about one another early on. Cleo Stockhoff, associate director of Talent Acquisition and Assessment at Verizon Wireless, said, "If people do not know one another, it is essential to try to get people together initially and perhaps even periodically in the first year. This initial investment goes a long way to building connectivity and trust."

Differentiator 5: Collaboration

The most successful virtual teams find ways to collaborate effectively and work together to achieve their collective goals. By contrast, members of less-effective teams often work on projects autonomously and may be less likely to collaborate to get work done.

Our study found that high-performing virtual teams scored significantly higher than low-performing virtual teams—an average of 3.35 compared to 2.92, respectively—on the Collaboration dimension (which means that members of high-performing teams tend to help one another and work together to achieve team goals).

When we looked more closely at the items in this dimension, we found that high-performing team members did a better job of supporting each other in goal achievement compared to members of low-performing teams, who tended to independently execute tasks and objectives (average of 3.50 compared to 3.02, respectively).

To collaborate effectively, we found that members of top-performing teams ensured they had a good understanding of one another's roles and responsibilities and that the team as a whole had clearly defined team objectives. They trusted one another to achieve objectives and had a process in place to communicate and share work.

The ShingleSeal Standstill: How Would You Handle It?

Next, we'll take a look at the RAMP model, which summarizes the key characteristics of effective virtual teams, and we'll offer some practical tips to improve virtual team performance. But first, let's assess how *you* would deal with a low-performing virtual team.

The case study below outlines one virtual team's performance challenges. Read the case and think about how you would handle it. After you complete it, use the scoring guidelines to evaluate how you did. Once you review the RAMP tips and guidelines for enhancing virtual team performance, we suggest revisiting the case to identify what you did well and to determine what you might do differently.

Case Study: ShingleSeal

ShingleSeal is a global manufacturing company that produces and distributes adhesives for roofing products. One of its major strategic initiatives for this year is to develop and implement a new customer management tracking system that will help the sales and production organizations keep up with client information and orders.

Rachel Phillips, the company's chief technology officer, was asked to pull together a dedicated team of IT programmers and specialists to handle this important initiative.

Three months ago, Rachel consulted each of her eight direct reports to identify the best resources for this project team. Because each of her direct reports wanted to have one of his or her team members on the team, Rachel decided to be more inclusive and ended up with thirty-four team members for the project. Fourteen of those members were located in ShingleSeal's corporate office in New Jersey, twelve members were located in its California office, and eight team members were scattered across various geographic locations around the world.

As the team leader, Rachel held a three-hour "virtual" kick-off meeting where team members from the New Jersey and California offices met via videoconferencing, and the remaining team members joined by telephone.

During this meeting, Rachel discussed the importance of the project, provided a high-level overview of the scope of work, and responded to team-member questions. After the meeting, the team was supposed to immediately get to work.

However, since the kick-off meeting two months ago, very little coordinated work has taken place. The team members in New Jersey often meet independently and the team members in California do the same, while the other team members are not involved in any of the day-to-day decisions. Because these two "sub-teams" are meeting independently to do work and are not involving others, they are duplicating work.

The project team meets on a weekly basis by telephone, but time zone differences often prevent the entire team from being in attendance at the same time. Rachel was too busy to attend the last team meeting and asked a team member to take over for her. During the meeting, team members in New Jersey recommended a technology platform for the new system, but team members in California had a totally different point of view and would not agree to move ahead unless the rest of the team considered *their* suggestion. A conflict ensued, which has now led to a standstill.

Rachel just received a call from one of the team members regarding what took place during the meeting and doesn't know what to do. Since you are a trusted peer, Rachel left you a voicemail asking for your advice on what steps she can take to enhance the effectiveness of her project team. What will you tell her? In crafting your recommendations, outline what Rachel might have done differently, as well as what next steps she should take to correct the team's problems.

Evaluating Your Responses

Check the factors below that you considered as you thought about how you would approach the situation.

❑ Review the size of the team—consider reducing the number of members from corporate and the California office. The team may be too large, contributing to a lack of clarity around roles.

❑ If the size of the team is reduced, think through how this will be communicated and how to identify who will remain on the team and who will not and why.

❑ Schedule a face-to-face meeting with all team members— conduct a "fun" team-building exercise to help build relationships.

❑ To select the best technology platform, engage the group in developing a list of objective decision criteria and evaluate the technology platform against that. Follow up with documentation of key decisions made—distribute to all team members.

❑ Identify a method for sharing documents and clarify expectations around communications (this can be discussed during the face-to-face team meeting).

❑ Clarify how decisions will be made within the team (that is, who needs to be involved in what kinds of decisions).

❑ Establish a weekly team video conferences with an agenda.

❑ Avoid delegating the role of the team leader—if necessary, ensure that the person taking the role of facilitator is clear about his or her responsibilities.

Use the guidelines in Table 4.1 below to determine how effectively you evaluated the case.

Table 4.1 Evaluating Your Responses

Number of Items Checked	Interpretation
6 or 7	You have considered the majority of the factors required to accelerate virtual team performance.
5	You have considered most of the factors required to accelerate virtual team performance.
4	You have considered some of the factors required to accelerate virtual team performance.
3	You have considered a few of the factors required to accelerate virtual team performance.

RAMP Up Virtual Team Performance

Based on our study findings on the differentiators of top-performing virtual teams, our experiences working directly with virtual teams, and the lessons we learned about why virtual teams fail, we developed the RAMP model. Designed to serve as a roadmap for virtual teams and their leaders, it provides practical steps to accelerate performance.

The model is comprised of four components that are critical to virtual team success: **R**elationships, **A**ccountability, **M**otivation, and **P**rocess and Purpose. For each component, in the following section we provide practical strategies that can be used to "ramp up" team performance.

RAMP Component 1: Relationships

Our research indicates that teams that focus solely on execution without attending to interpersonal relationships are not as effective. Top-performing teams had an average score of 3.42 on the Interpersonal Relationships dimension of our survey, compared to an average of 3.04 in low-performing teams.

Because virtual team members are working together from a distance and cannot collaborate face-to-face, in order to be successful they must find other ways to form quality relationships. There are three facets of effective virtual relationships: communication, trust, and effective conflict resolution. Let's take a look.

Communication. To work together effectively, virtual team members must provide one another with necessary information and respond to each other in a timely manner. The most effective virtual teams establish a communication protocol that outlines how members will communicate. This protocol delineates which technologies the team prefers and when they will use them. They typically have a shared online workspace where team members can share ideas and information and post team documents.

The most effective virtual teams match the technology to the task. For example, they may use instant messaging for quick questions or "real-time" updates, email for brief exchanges of information, and videoconferencing or webinars for group discussions and brainstorming sessions.

Of course, each method of communication has its pros and cons. Email is a great way to share information, but is often less useful for creating a two-way dialogue. It also leaves the door open for miscommunications when messages are misinterpreted, especially when it is used by team members from different cultures. Teleconferences are also good ways to share information, but some of the best virtual teams also use that time to promote a two-way dialogue.

Communication is even more of a challenge in cross-cultural teams on which different backgrounds, cultural norms, and language barriers may exist. In cross-cultural teams on which there are non-native English-speaking team members, it is especially important to ensure there are processes in place to promote discussion and overcome any communication barriers.

Many of the low-performing teams haven't taken the time to set up shared communication practices and often fail to use the most appropriate technology to accomplish their goals. We've found that virtual teams that neglect other elements and focus too much on technology and not enough on how to use it appropriately typically run into performance problems.

Trust. Naturally, trust is critical when it comes to building strong relationships. However, building trust in a virtual setting can be a real challenge, especially in highly diverse teams.

Zaccaro and Bader[3] contend that development and maintenance of trust may be one of the most important factors for virtual team success. There's simply no quicker way to stifle performance than by having team members who don't trust each other and, as a result, aren't willing to work together on certain issues. Lack of trust can quickly damage the dynamics of a virtual team.

Virtual team members can build trust by communicating openly and honestly, modeling positive behaviors, implementing a communication plan for team interactions, and being accessible and responsive. Trust will likely take longer to build for virtual teams than for co-located ones, so it's important that they focus on this element from day one.

We highly recommend an initial team face-to-face meeting within the first thirty days of working together so that members can get to know one another and begin developing relationships. In situations when face-to-face meetings aren't possible, teams should leverage online tools such as group video conferencing, web-based video, instant messaging, and Facebook-like web pages with personal profiles and pictures so that team members can become acquainted and learn about each other's backgrounds and experiences. In addition, having a task-based focus with clearly defined goals early on also helps virtual teams to develop trust.[4]

Conflict Resolution. Our research shows that top-performing virtual teams know how to effectively manage differences and reach agreement. These teams scored significantly higher on the prompt "Team members handle conflict in an appropriate manner" than their low-performing counterparts (3.27 compared to 2.92).

In addition, we found that learning to more effectively resolve conflicts was the one change that would significantly improve the performance of less-effective teams.

No matter how well a team's members get along, or how clear the team's goals are, differences of opinion are going to pop up, especially in stressful situations. The same elements that cause conflict in co-located teams—different communication styles, varying skill levels, and different perspectives on how to handle problems—will cause conflict for virtual teams. But virtual teams face other challenges as well. In a virtual environment, for instance, it's more common for people to misinterpret what someone has said or come to the wrong conclusions because of the way he or she said something.

It's also common for team members to avoid dealing with potential conflicts in a timely manner because of the low frequency of direct contact or the difficulties of constructively talking about differences via phone or email.

That said, when differences of opinion arise, team members need to know how to react to one another. When they have the appropriate skills to identify and resolve conflict, they are able to handle disagreements constructively and will ultimately find the best solutions for team and company problems.

The following tips will help virtual team members enhance communication, build trust, and effectively manage conflict:

- Focus on both the task and the interpersonal and social processes. Make an effort to speak informally with colleagues on a regular basis. Doing so will help you compensate for the lack of face-to-face contact and will help you build trust and team spirit.

- Create a shared web-based space for informal team communication so members have the opportunity to create personal relationships and decrease feelings of isolation. For example, to help increase engagement and social interaction, some organizations have created "virtual water coolers" and team websites and/or have provided instant messaging capability to encourage team communication.

- Ensure that you are comfortable raising issues and giving feedback to other team members over the phone. Remember, when first raising or addressing a difference of opinion or perspective, don't use email. However, it is okay to use email to confirm your understanding of what was said over the phone.

- Recognize that conflicts are neither good nor bad in and of themselves. Outcomes may be positive or negative, but conflicts are not. They are merely differences of opinion and will be present in even the best-performing teams and among people who get along very well.

- When a conflict occurs, clarify the situation by identifying the individuals involved in the conflict, defining the issues specifically, and gathering facts and perceptions of the people involved.
- The seven-step process outlined below for managing conflict can be applied to most situations:
  1. Describe what's important to you and why it is important.
  2. Check your understanding of what's important to the other person and why it is important.
  3. Identify common ground and look for points of interdependence.
  4. Invite alternatives that address your needs/goals and the other person's needs/goals.
  5. Use active listening (paraphrase, questions, balanced response) to evaluate alternatives, resolve concerns, and improve ideas.
  6. If an alternative isn't immediately available, temporarily remove constraints to invite and propose new alternatives.
  7. End the discussion by summarizing key points and stating next steps.
- Focus on the problem, not the person. Try to see problems from both sides. If the situation heats up, stay with the facts and avoid personal issues.
- Deal with conflicts right away. Letting them fester will only lead to more problems, especially in a virtual setting.
- Experiment with different ways of staying in contact. Determine which methods are most effective with specific individuals.
- Make it easy for your team members to reach you. Establish set times that you would be available for conference calls or video conferencing.
- When the virtual team is first formed, spend time learning about team members' personalities, cultural backgrounds, and work habits.

- Ensure that you don't respond to messages or problems when you are overly emotional, tired, or upset.

- Select the appropriate technology or way to communicate when there are problems or conflicts. For example, things can easily be taken out of context in email, so the telephone might be better.

- Understand that cultural differences (national, geographic, gender, age, and functional) may exist between team members. And remember that learning about team members' cultures in terms of language, views on time management, the importance of socialization, and what may be considered offensive will enhance communication between team members.

RAMP Component 2: Accountability

Top-performing companies also have better methods for holding employees accountable for their work. Our research indicates that 77 percent of leaders in top-performing organizations report that employees are held accountable for results, compared to only 44 percent in less-successful organizations.

Accountability is even more challenging in a virtual setting. Mark Feurer, director of Global HR Planning and Development at Bunge, explains, "Accountability is very important. Many virtual team members have their own day-to-day work plus the work they have to do on an integrated team, so this often leads to a lack of accountability. This can impede productivity and the focus of the team, since many leaders do not address performance issues and conflicts."

What are some of the indicators of a lack of accountability? One is the you're-not-going-to-pin-this-on-me mentality by which employees use evasion and avoidance tactics to escape blame for failed initiatives or tasks.

You might also see reduced innovation and risk taking. In a low-accountability environment, people are simply less willing to think outside the proverbial box and risk presenting an idea or solution that could go wrong and result in an onslaught of blame. There's also a tendency for team meetings to turn into "blamestorming" sessions where members point fingers at one another for group problems. Finally, there's a shutdown in communications, especially about those things that go wrong.

Why do some team members try so hard to avoid accountability? Research on excuse-making indicates that there are several factors that explain why people deny involvement when things go wrong, blame others, or explain why things were beyond their control. Developing an understanding of these factors provides the foundation for being able to effectively manage accountability in ourselves and others. The factors include preservation of self-image, social loafing, and locus of control. Let's take a closer look at each of these factors.

Preservation of Self-Image. Most people think of themselves as superior to others in areas that are important to them, such as intelligence, creativity, or various technical skills. We are also generally motivated to present ourselves favorably to others. When our self-image is threatened, we take measures to maintain it, including taking credit for success and disavowing failures.

Research has found that we also tend to shift the reasons for negative outcomes to sources that are less threatening to our self-image. For example, instead of saying, "I didn't complete the project on time because I have poor project management skills" one might say, "I didn't complete the project on time because I couldn't get the information I needed from another team member." Although the latter excuse still acknowledges participation in creating the problem, it minimizes the team member's direct responsibility and focuses on a cause that is less threatening to his or her self-image.

"Social Loafing." Social loafing is a phrase that explains why individual effort decreases as team size increases.[5] Social loafing

can be especially problematic in large virtual teams, where there is often decreased role clarity and a lack of ownership of tasks. What leads to social loafing? The main catalyst may center on identifiability. For example, the stakes are higher when people know their decisions or actions will be attributable to them and that they have to justify themselves and their actions to others.

Consider a research study that examined the impact of identifiability on swimmers.[6] The researchers found that swimmers recorded better times in relays than in individual races when their performance was identifiable. However, their performance was worse when they were not identifiable (that is, when they knew their individual lap times would not be made public). In other words, when the swimmers knew they could "hide" in the team, they tended to slack off a little more than when they were being judged on their own merits.

This notion of identifiability may be further exacerbated in a virtual environment, where it may be more difficult to identify the exact nature of team members' contributions. As a result, the individual efforts of team members may decrease on virtual teams, particularly larger teams when it becomes even harder to identify individual contributions and monitor performance. Team members know they can "loaf" and get away with it.

Locus of Control. We all fall somewhere along the locus of control continuum, which might be summed up as follows: Do you believe that your destiny and behavior is guided by your personal decisions and efforts or do you believe it's guided by fate, luck, or other external circumstances?

When you believe you control your own destiny and determine your own direction, you have an internal locus of control. Such people tend to work harder and persevere longer in order to get what they want. They believe hard work and personal abilities will lead to positive outcomes. They also tend to engage in activities that will improve their situations and try to figure out why things turned out the way they did. Because they believe they control their destiny, they're less inclined to make excuses and more inclined to take accountability for their actions and the resulting consequence.

People with an external locus of control, on the other hand, believe that what happens to them is the result of circumstances that are beyond their control. As a result, they are usually more prone to make excuses and to avoid being held accountable for their actions.

What does a culture of accountability look like in virtual teams? Those that get accountability right are disciplined and follow through on every commitment and initiative (or make a conscious decision to drop commitments that are wasting time or that will have negative outcomes). These teams tolerate honest mistakes and, when problems arise, members engage in creative problem solving rather than rationalizing and justifying shortfalls.

In addition, everyone takes full responsibility for his or her actions and outcomes and counts on others rather than trying to escape blame. There are no surprises, as people are open and honest about problems. Finally, team members hold one another accountable for their decisions and actions.

Some virtual teams operate like self-managed work teams (SMWTs), or self-directed teams, where members collaborate and hold one another accountable for meeting shared commitments. For example, SMWTs do not have formal leaders. Instead team members rotate in and out of the leadership position depending on the project or task.

Effective SMWTs have high levels of coordination and efficiency, establish performance goals that are monitored over time, and provide regular feedback and communication.[7] Some virtual teams may not require formal leadership. If they don't, it is a good idea to apply the SMWT principles to their teamwork.

A recent article in *MIT Sloan Management Review*[8] presents the idea that those chosen to be on virtual teams need to be more self-sufficient at managing their work because it can be challenging for a leader to assume that role for employees who are not co-located. The article's authors assert that it is critical to promote self-leadership across the team, which increases accountability among team members. Based on what we saw in our study, the authors of the article hit the nail on the head. We found that having team members who were willing to take on additional leadership responsibility as needed was a critical performance differentiator.

Ever heard the phrase "What gets measured gets done"? It's true. And that's why both leaders and members of virtual teams should incorporate one or more activities related to their roles on the team into their annual objectives or personal development plans. For example, some of the top-performing virtual teams in our study set up several different metrics to assess their teams' performances over time. Some of the metrics—such as efficiency, quality, and customer satisfaction—are quantifiable and generally easy to track.

It's also important that teams focus on a few critical metrics that are mutually supportive rather than numerous metrics that can lead to incompatible demands. Not only will this ensure individuals are motivated for team success, but it will also encourage them to use team participation as a growth and development mechanism to improve their skills.

Tips to enhance accountability include:

- Ensure you understand each team member's role and your role related to team decisions and activities.
- Set people up for success by clarifying expectations, who's accountable, and the due date for a task of assignment.
- If you are not clear about expectations, check in and ask.
- Develop an action plan that outlines key activities, accountabilities, and due dates and use it to manage and monitor progress.

- Have regular calls or check-in meetings to review progress on team goals or deliverables. Don't wait until the due date to check in. Check in periodically before it's too late to make any course corrections.

- Keep your promises and commitments. As soon as you realize that you cannot meet a commitment, let team members know and solicit their advice to get things done.

- Be willing to ask for and receive help. Acknowledging that you may not be able to or have the time to carry out a particular responsibility, but not discussing it with team members, could delay progress and cause conflict among the team members.

- Establish processes to periodically monitor virtual team performance to determine whether the team is functioning efficiently and effectively.

- Offer support and resources to help team members who may require assistance.

- When a deadline is missed or a commitment is not met, instead of looking to affix blame, ask and encourage people to ask three "accountability questions": *What did I do that might have contributed to this problem? What can I do to get things back on track? What can I do to prevent this from happening again?*

RAMP Component 3: Motivation

Our research indicates that high-performing virtual teams are more motivated than less-effective teams. Top-performing teams had an average score of 3.64 on the "Team Motivation" dimension, compared to an average of 3.18 for low-performing teams.

Specifically, members of high-performing teams demonstrate a high level of initiative and are willing to put in extra effort to achieve team objectives. They work together and help one another achieve goals. And they are willing to step up and assume leadership responsibility when needed.

Why are some teams extremely motivated while others lack motivation? Our research shows that three key factors can lead to increased motivation for virtual teams:

- Team members help one another accomplish shared objectives. They work together effectively and respond quickly when problems arise.
- The team effectively handles team conflict rather than ignore issues and conflicts that exist between team members.
- Team members understand how the team's work contributes to the success of the organization.

Alignment between individual goals, team goals, and broader organizational goals is an important component of engagement and motivation, and these elements play out in our study findings. We also know that team leadership plays an important role in creating and maintaining high levels of motivation.

Think of someone who is good at motivating others. What behaviors does that person demonstrate? Is he or she visible, approachable, and engaged and therefore perceived by the team as someone who is "willing to get in the foxhole" when needed? If the person is truly a great motivator, then your answer will be yes.

Effective motivators are able to create purpose and meaning for people's work. They understand why people behave as they do and know what motivates different individuals. Effective motivators also reinforce positive behavior and recognize individuals and teams for their accomplishments.

Motivating team members from a distance is even more challenging. Quite simply, it's hard to determine how to motivate individuals you may never have met or know only at a superficial level, and it is difficult to inspire people when you are not face-to-face. Our research corroborates these factors. We find that top-performing virtual team leaders are able to inspire team members to do their best, whereas leaders of less-effective teams weren't able to do so.

Although the leader may be primarily responsible for motivating the team, team members can and should motivate one another. Strategies to help motivate virtual team members include:

- Brand your team. Create a group identity by developing a team name, slogan, logo, or other insignia. Team branding can be a great way to establish strong group identification and even team pride.
- Take time at the beginning or end of a team call to review team and individual successes and accomplishments.
- Get to know what motivates each member of the team (affiliation, accomplishment, independence, safety, power, etc.) and try to assign work that aligns with those factors.
- Conduct periodic face-to-face meetings or use technologies, such as video conferencing, to engage and motivate team members.
- Treat people as you expect to be treated. Communicate openly, honestly, and often.
- Frequently recognize successes and make them visible, especially when other team members have significant achievements. For example, spotlight team accomplishments in a company/department virtual newsletter or on its intranet site.
- Set challenging performance expectations that require people to stretch and pick up new skills and knowledge.
- Provide interesting assignments that are outside the normal work routine (make sure these types of assignments are given to everyone on the team not just given to the one or two people you like the best or trust the most).

- Reinforce the team's sense of purpose by periodically reminding team members how what they are doing relates to the "big picture."

- Identify and remove obstacles that make it difficult to get the work done.

- Involve team members in decisions that affect them by asking for their input and soliciting their feedback.

RAMP Component 4: Process and Purpose

The most effective virtual teams establish clear goals, roles, and processes from the start. Taking the time to do so is critical for team success. In our study, high-performing virtual teams were better at defining clear roles and responsibilities than less-effective teams were. (High-performing teams averaged 3.24 compared to 2.80.)

The *MIT Sloan Management Review*[9] study supports our finding that establishing team processes is critical for high performance. Specifically, the study found that the key performance drivers are specific, task-related team processes that help coordinate work among team members or facilitate communication among members. Interestingly, the research also indicates that virtual teams that implement such processes outperform their co-located counterparts.

Successful virtual teams are very clear about how their work contributes to the success of the organization. In contrast, we have spoken to people serving on less-effective teams who openly admit that their team has no purpose and who question how it benefits their organization. When asked about this lack of a broader purpose, a team member on a global human resources team said, "It would be helpful to hear about strategic plans rather than being so focused on the execution of projects and tasks that seem disconnected."

The following tips will help establish clear processes and goals for your virtual team:

- Develop operating guidelines to help structure virtual team communication and coordination. For example, you might set meeting schedules and establish rules of engagement that outline how and when members speak with one another. If your team members are located in different time zones, rotate meeting times so that the same team members do not consistently have to take calls late at night or early in the morning to participate.

- To clarify who is held accountable for what, identify team member roles and responsibilities. Revisit these roles and responsibilities regularly to determine whether they should be revised as goals and priorities evolve.

- Obtain team agreement on objectives and the strategies that will lead to attaining them.

- Ensure the team has adequate resources to successfully accomplish its goals.

- Set up a process to assess whether or not the team is communicating and collaborating effectively and what it can do differently to be even more effective in these areas.

- Use the Internet or work-group calendaring software to store team members' calendars. While this could be difficult to maintain on a daily basis, it should not be difficult to keep up with scheduled out-of-town absences such as vacations or business travel.

For existing teams, the RAMP Model can be used to assess progress and identify performance barriers. If you are about to launch a new virtual team, be sure to frequently review these factors using the Quick Reference Guide (Table 4.2) and also be sure to frequently assess your progress in these key areas.

Table 4.2 Quick Reference Guide

Problem	Solutions
Team members are not effectively collaborating with one another.	• Identify what deliverables the team needs to work together on and develop a plan to ensure that team members work on tasks jointly. • Clarify shared team goals and each person's role in achieving those goals. • Ensure roles and decision authority are clear and agreed to—make sure people know what to expect from each other. • Assess what barriers are preventing communication and collaboration. For example, does the team have the technology they need to easily collaborate with one another? • Once a plan is in place, set milestones to periodically assess performance.
There seems to be a lack of trust.	• Take time to assess what factors are leading to the lack of trust. Is there a problem between certain team members or subgroups? • Ensure the structural elements required for teamwork are in place (shared goals, clear roles, and processes for decision making). Lack of trust is frequently an unintended consequence when these factors are not in place and people consistently disappoint each other or "bump into" each other. • If appropriate, have a candid discussion with individual team members or the team as a whole to discuss how the team will move forward. • Ensure that team members have time to build relationships with one another.

Table 4.2 (*Continued*)

Problem	*Solutions*

The team is not meeting its commitments.	• Take time to diagnose what is getting in the way of effective execution.
	• Consider the following:
	  – Does the team have clear goals with due dates and assigned responsibilities?
	  – Do team members have clear roles?
	  – Are team members being held accountable?
	  – Are sufficient resources available?
	  – Are priorities clear and agreed on?
	  – Are due dates realistic given the available resources?
	  – Are people stretched too thinly (on too many teams, trying to please too many bosses)?

There are conflicts between individuals or groups of individuals.	• When a conflict occurs, it is important to clarify the situation by identifying the individuals involved in the conflict, defining the issues creating the conflict, and gathering facts and perceptions of the people involved. Use a seven-step process for managing conflict: 1. Describe what's important to you and why it is important. 2. Check your understanding of what's important to the other person and why it is important. 3. Identify common ground and look for points of interdependence. 4. Invite alternatives that address your needs/goals and the other person's needs/goals. 5. Use active listening (paraphrase, questions, balanced response) to evaluate alternatives, resolve concerns, and improve ideas.

(*continued overleaf*)

Table 4.2 (Continued)

Problem	Solutions
	6. If an alternative isn't immediately available, temporarily remove constraints to invite and propose new alternatives.
	7. End the discussion by summarizing key points and stating next steps.
The team seems to have several "subgroups" or factions based on geographic location.	• Bring the issue to the entire team for discussion.
	• Ask people to assess their level of collaboration (what is working well and what they could do differently to be more effective).
	• Discuss the impact of silos on the team's work.

Conclusion

Most virtual teams face the same performance hurdles. But not all virtual teams successfully overcome them. Some teams fail simply because they are not aware of what it takes to perform well in a virtual environment.

Our study has helped close this knowledge gap for virtual teams. It identifies the five differentiators of virtual team performance: *achieving commitment and engagement, effectively sharing decision-making processes, getting the right information to the right people at the right time,* and *collaborating to achieve team objectives.* With this information, leaders and organizations can take the steps necessary for improving their virtual teams' performance levels.

In other cases, virtual teams fail to perform because their leaders and team members don't know how to overcome the challenges associated with working virtually. In these situations, as we've discussed in this chapter, the RAMP Model provides specific guidelines and actions for enhancing a team's performance in four areas related to team success: *relationships*, *accountability*, *motivation*, and *processes and purpose*.

The Bottom Line

To compensate for the lack of face-to-face contact, successful virtual teams emphasize the interpersonal dynamics of virtual collaboration and establish practices for building trust, increasing transparency, and enhancing interpersonal relationships.

Section Two

Leading Virtual Teams

Chapter Five

How to Lead Virtual Teams—Tips, Techniques, and Best Practices for High Performance

"Out of sight, foremost in mind. How do you
manage people whom you don't see regularly?"

—*Charles Handy*[1]

We've already established that quality leadership is essential for a virtual team's success. And that it's not an easy job. Virtual team leaders face challenges similar to those of leaders of co-located teams. However, for the former, many of those challenges are exacerbated by distance and time zone differences.

As Jay Moldenhauer-Salazar, vice president of talent management at Gap, Inc., suggests, "The things that are good for virtual teams are the same as with traditional teams, but they become even more important in virtual teams."

However, virtual team leaders also face some challenges all their own.

Challenges Virtual Team Leaders Face

In OnPoint's study, we asked 150 virtual team leaders to identify the top challenges they face when leading from a distance. They pinpointed the following challenges as the greatest barriers to their performance: *infrequent face-to-face contact, lack of resources, difficulties in building a collaborative atmosphere virtually, lack of time to focus on leading the team, shifting team and organizational priorities,* and *difficulties in managing poor performers.* Let's explore them further.

Challenge 1: Infrequent Face-to-Face Contact

OnPoint's study, which surveyed virtual team leaders and team members, focused on the primary challenges that virtual teams commonly face. Infrequent face-to-face contact was the top challenge reported by team members and—perhaps not surprisingly—43 percent of the leaders in our study concurred.

Even though leaders recognize that these challenges come with the territory when working virtually, they still often struggle to fully overcome them. Virtual team leaders report that the lack of face-to-face contact makes it tougher to build trust within their teams, engage their teams, and monitor their team members' work.

Mark Gasta, senior vice president and chief human resource officer of Vail Resorts, believes these challenges require leaders to change their approach when managing virtually. "To expect that you can build trust and relationships on a conference call is naïve," Gasta says. "Simple things are important. Calling on your way home just to say hello and check in with people can have a big impact. It is like popping into people's offices if they were on-site. You need to figure out how to apply the same type of behaviors effective team leaders do when they are face-to-face."

Challenge 2: Lack of Resources

Thirty-nine percent of leaders reported challenges associated with a lack of resources. And although co-located teams must also deal with this problem, virtual team leaders frequently suffer from the lack of a specific type of resource—technology.

Since virtual teams do not meet in person around a conference table, they must have the technology to effectively communicate and transfer information. It's not optional. And yet many teams are forced to make do without it.

One leader reported that it was difficult to gain access to his company's TelePresence (a video conferencing technology) room, which was frequently booked months in advance. Other leaders were not able to use instant messaging because of company policy or videoconferencing because of restrictive security and firewalls—even though both technologies would have enhanced their teams' effectiveness.

In addition, many teams lack the resources to cover travel expenses so they could periodically meet in person, a practice that would help them compensate for their technology shortfalls.

Challenge 3: Difficulty Building a Collaborative Atmosphere Virtually

How do you create a high-touch, interactive environment when you are not physically present with your team? How can you build an atmosphere of collaboration and cooperation? Achieving these factors can be especially challenging when you have a large virtual team and must work around time zone differences.

At the heart of this problem lies a fundamental question: *Are human beings more inclined to be cooperative or competitive?* As with most matters of human behavior, the answers aren't always clear-cut. There is plenty of disagreement on the subject.

Economic and rational choice theory point to our competitive nature and a propensity to put our own self-interest ahead of the well-being of the group. Of course, not everyone behaves the way economic and game theory models predict. In fact, there is evidence that people cooperate more often than theories of self-interest and maximizing personal benefit might suggest.

Many social scientists believe that cooperation may be society's more natural state.[2] This idea derives from the fact that for much of our history we lived in hunter and gatherer societies, which tend to support cooperation for both efficiency and for maximizing individual good.

However, research has found that, although cooperation may initially be a more common response, it seems that we are quicker to stop cooperating than we are to stop competing. And once cooperation has stopped, it takes longer for us to forgive and trust in order to resume cooperating.[3]

With self-interest and the fragility of cooperation working against you, encouraging and sustaining cooperation and collaboration in a virtual team environment is a daunting challenge. However, it is not an insurmountable one.

Gasta uses a strategy to help enhance collaboration in his virtual HR team: "One technique that I use is to break the team into smaller sub-teams called passion groups, which are areas people are interested in," he reports. "The larger team then becomes a steering committee that provides ownership and ensures the sub-teams stay connected."

Group size isn't the only critical factor. There are certain conditions in which cooperation is more likely to trump competition—namely, when communication is clear, when transparency exists, when people understand what they can expect from the other person and how they will work together, and when the interests of individuals or groups are aligned. We'll say more about what you can do to create and sustain an environment that supports collaboration later in the chapter.

Challenge 4: Lack of Time to Focus on Leading the Team

As we've mentioned before, team membership and team leadership are responsibilities that employees often take on in addition to their daily work. Consequently, team leaders are already pulled in multiple directions and have little time to effectively manage their virtual teams.

In many cases, virtual team leaders may be managing several teams (or are members of several teams), which can be both time-consuming and overwhelming. In our interviews, we frequently heard examples of leaders who had more work than they could handle. This reality, coupled with the fact that many team members are stretched too thin as well, often leads to missed deadlines and a lack of productivity.

Tom, a virtual team leader, indicated, "I really do not have the time to focus on this virtual team, yet there is no one else to take over. Unfortunately, this negatively impacts the team's ability to achieve its goals."

Challenge 5: Shifting Team and Organizational Priorities

While some virtual team leaders communicate goals up-front, they may neglect to update them as priorities shift. According to Moldenhauer-Salazar, "The financial services industry has been highly dynamic, so it is much harder to communicate information and keep people informed about changes and decisions. This becomes particularly challenging when you are leading a geographically dispersed team."

A common complaint from team members is that they aren't properly informed about changes in priorities and goals. One person we interviewed stated, "Our leader does not make sure that we know about changes to initiatives that affect our work, which is very frustrating. We often waste time and resources because we were not aware of a change."

Another team member indicated, "My team leader does a better job updating team members who are in the same geographic location as he is, but he neglects to communicate key changes to team members in other locations."

Challenge 6: Difficulty Managing Poor Performers

In addition to our study on virtual teams, OnPoint recently conducted a survey of over four hundred leaders. Forty percent of them reported that employees in their organizations are not being held accountable for results. In addition, 20 percent reported that managers in their organizations don't deal with poor performers.

So why don't leaders deal with performance issues? One of the most common reasons leaders fail to hold team members account-able is that they don't effectively communicate expectations—or for that matter, what "good" behaviors or deliverables even look like.

In addition, when leading a team of people who are geo-graphically distributed, timely feedback also poses a challenge. Time zone differences or infrequent contact can increase the "lag time" between when the problem occurs, when the leader becomes aware of the problem, and when the opportunity to provide feedback arises.

Conflict avoidance is another reason. Many leaders would rather attempt to wait out a problem than risk getting into a potentially contentious conversation with a team member.

And dealing with poor performers is particularly difficult when you can't regularly observe your team members. How can virtual team leaders regularly monitor team members' work when they have limited or no physical contact? To make matters worse, how can a virtual team leader provide timely feedback and/or hold team members accountable when leading a team whose members do not report directly to him or her?

Raygen Company Slump: How Would You Handle It?

Before we introduce the factors that separate the best virtual team leaders from the rest of the pack and provide some practical tips for enhancing your effectiveness, take a few minutes to assess how you would deal with a virtual team that is having performance problems.

Read the following case study and think about how you would handle it. Write down how you would approach each situation. After you complete that process, use the scoring guidelines to evaluate how you did. Then when you've reviewed the tips and guidelines for leading from a distance, revisit the case study to determine what you might do differently.

Case Study: Raygen Company

Raygen Company is a global professional services firm that provides consulting services to its clients. One key to Raygen's success is its innovative marketing strategies.

Three years ago, the SVP of marketing formed a cross-functional virtual team made up of ten geographically dispersed employees from marketing, sales, consulting, and finance. Throughout this three-year period, the team was extremely successful in generating and implementing new marketing strategies.

However, it appears as though the team has hit a plateau in terms of its performance. Both the quality and the timeliness of the team's deliverables seem to have declined over the past several months. While performance isn't currently below standard, it *is* mediocre—something that this team never seemed to tolerate in the past.

Ted Jones, the current team leader, has announced that he will be leaving the organization next month and has asked that you step in, at least on an interim basis, to fill his role. In addition to describing the team's current performance issues, Ted explains that its members are busy with other job responsibilities and do not seem to be fully engaged with the team.

In order to prepare for your new leadership role, you'll be meeting with Ted to review your initial ideas for enhancing the team's performance. What ideas do you have?

Evaluating Your Response

Check each of the factors listed below that you considered as possible solutions:

❑ Conduct a face-to-face (ideally) or telephone interview with each team member to solicit their opinions on what factors are currently supporting or inhibiting teamwork.

❑ Distribute a brief, anonymous survey to all team members to collect data on what factors support or inhibit team work—summarize data and distribute it to team members to facilitate a discussion around key strengths and areas for improvement.

❏ Solicit input from team members about how to measure and monitor progress against goals (ideally during a face-to-face meeting).

❏ Review and prioritize shared goals with the team.

❏ Clarify performance expectations for each team member. Ensure individual goals and priorities are aligned with team goals and supported by all team members.

❏ Acknowledge the team's track record for success and express confidence that performance will improve in the future.

❏ Review how team and individual performance are being recognized and rewarded to ensure alignment with desired behaviors.

❏ Proactively manage the change associated with a new team leader—create forums for team members to express their concerns, ask questions, and share information.

Use the guidelines in Table 5.1 below to determine how effectively you evaluated the case.

Table 5.1 Evaluating Your Responses

Number of Items Checked	Interpretation
6 to 8	You have considered the majority of the factors required to successfully lead a virtual team.
5	You have considered most of the factors required to successfully lead a virtual team.
4	You have considered some of the factors required to successfully lead a virtual team.
3	You have considered a few of the factors required to successfully lead a virtual team.

Virtual Team Leadership Self-Assessment

Before we talk about what it takes to be an effective virtual team leader, assess your own level of effectiveness. Read each item in Exhibit 5.1 and, using the rating scale provided, consider how each item describes your behavior as a virtual team leader.

Exhibit 5.1. Virtual Team Leader Self-Assessment

1 = Never	2 = Sometimes	3 = Almost All of the Time

Item	Rating
1. Take steps to foster collaboration among team members.	
2. Ensure that there are adequate resources to support the team.	
3. Delegate work effectively to team members.	
4. Empower team members to make decisions.	
5. Resolve team conflict effectively.	
6. Inspire team members to do their best.	
7. Respond quickly when problems arise.	
8. Provide timely feedback to team members.	
9. Provide coaching and support to team members.	
10. Hold team members accountable.	

How well did you do? If you scored between 25 and 30, you have a good handle on what it takes to lead a virtual team. If you scored between 10 and 20, you may not be using as many of these key strategies as consistently as you should.

In the next section we'll discuss the factors that differentiate the most effective virtual team leaders. Compare yourself to this profile to better understand how well prepared you are to lead a virtual team (even if you scored above 25 on the self-assessment).

What Makes an Effective Virtual Team Leader?

We asked virtual team members, leaders, and stakeholders (customers or recipients of the team's output) what they believed were the most important competencies for a virtual team leader. They overwhelmingly selected communication as the most important skill required for success.

Gasta agrees, "Communication is essential for leaders and is also a critical success factor. Leaders need to create a two-way conversation that keeps people engaged."

Building relationships, building trust, being personally accountable, and being results-driven were also cited among the top competencies. Team members and leaders also chose the ability to motivate others and action planning as being important, whereas stakeholders identified coaching and strategic thinking as key competencies for team leaders.

While these characteristics are perceived as being important for virtual team leader effectiveness, we wanted to determine which behaviors are directly connected to highly effective virtual team leadership. However, we did not seek to compare virtual team leaders to co-located team members. Instead, our objective was to understand what separates the most effective virtual team leaders from the least effective.

In general, we found that the most effective virtual team leaders are able to balance execution-oriented practices with the interpersonal, communication, and cultural factors critical to the success of virtual teams. Specifically, we found that the following five practices separated the most effective leaders from the least effective: *the ability to effectively manage change, the ability to foster an atmosphere of collaboration, the ability to communicate team goals and direction, strong interpersonal communication skills,* and *the ability to empower team members.*

Differentiator 1: Ability to Effectively Manage Change

Managing change and leading teams through transitions is particularly difficult when team members are geographically dispersed. Top-performing virtual team leaders had an average score of 4.2, based on a 5-point scale ranging from "Poor" to "Outstanding," on their ability to effectively manage change, whereas low-performing team leaders scored a 3.47.

The most effective leaders develop a process for helping their teams adjust to change. They are also sure to involve team members in decisions that affect them. Doing so increases the quality of the team's decision making and helps maintain high levels of enthusiasm and commitment for the duration of the change. The most effective team leaders use a three-step process for managing change, described below.

Step 1: Envisioning Change. Articulating a vision of what your team needs to accomplish helps to communicate the importance of change initiatives in a way that's understandable, meaningful, and inspiring. A variety of elements may be included in the vision, such as strategic objectives, key values for the company or team, general approaches for attaining the vision, slogans and symbols, and a description of what the vision will mean to people when it is attained.

In times of great change, people look to their leaders for direction. That's why it's essential to communicate personal confidence that the vision can be achieved and that the benefits will be worth the short-term sacrifices—a task that's more difficult when you have limited in-person contact with your team. Therefore, it's important that leaders convey a message of confidence and optimism by consistently demonstrating their conviction and support of the vision.

Step 2: Building Support for Change. Although most people would agree that change is essential if an organization is to adapt, grow, and remain competitive, the process often produces anxiety and resistance within organizational teams.

Many of us try to convince people to change by asserting our views and trying to talk the person out of his or her viewpoint. But this approach rarely works. Direct argument, in fact, often causes the other person to more vigorously support his or her position. A reflective and empathetic style, rather than an authoritative one, seems to be the most effective approach when we want someone to change his or her behavior.[4]

To help people deal with their resistance to a change, effective virtual team leaders encourage people to make the arguments for change themselves. This self-persuasive dialogue is called "change talk."[5]

Change talk encourages people to talk about their confidence in their ability to change, their desire to change, the importance of change, and their reasons to change. When people engage in this type of discussion, they are more likely to achieve higher levels of readiness to change than when the leader explains the reasons or advantages to them.[6]

For people to support change, they must see it as necessary and feasible. Virtual team leaders can build such support by discussing the urgent need for change, creating a broad coalition of supporters, identifying likely opponents and reasons for their resistance, and taking action to deal with resistance.

Step 3: Implementing Change. It's impossible to anticipate all the potential problems that could arise during a major change initiative or to prepare detailed plans for carrying out every aspect of the change. Perhaps surprisingly, a change is less likely to be successful if a leader tries to dictate in detail how it will be implemented. That's because involving others in decisions helps ensure we have access to information and perspectives that might not otherwise be available to us and decreases the likelihood that we'll take irrational action or make choices based solely on the familiarity of the situation ("I've seen this before and I know what needs to be done"). In addition, involving others increases decision acceptance, which is critical to effective execution once the decision has been made.

When a change is underway, effective leaders fill key positions with competent change agents, help people adjust to and cope with the change, provide opportunities to celebrate early successes, keep people informed about the progress of the change, and ensure that they demonstrate continued commitment to the change.

Following are a few general tips to help virtual leaders manage change:

- Express enthusiasm for the benefits of the change and confidence that the change will improve the current situation.

- Identify the people whose commitment is essential to the change effort and involve them in making key decisions.

- Identify people who might resist the change effort and make a special effort to bring them on board. Involve them in planning and in identifying and solving potential problems.

- Engage in two-way communication throughout the change by holding conference calls with the team or making yourself available for phone conversations with individual team members. Balance "telling" and "informing" with "asking."

- Encourage people to talk about why they think the change is important and how confident they are about making the change. Use this information to determine their level of readiness and what approach to take to move them to the next level.

- Discuss what will change and when it will change, what team members will need to do differently, and what you will do differently.

- Make the change objectives concrete by clarifying what the change looks like in terms of behavior and performance expectations.

Differentiator 2: Ability to Foster an Atmosphere of Collaboration

Effective virtual team leaders are able to use strategies to make up for the lack of human contact. They continually look for new ways to infuse team spirit and trust into their teams and to boost productivity.

Zeller stated, "I have realized that I put much more emphasis on building trust and relationships with others. This is much harder to do when you are working virtually. I also have to be purposeful about this since I am a task-first type of person, so I need to focus on trust."

The high-performing leaders in our study had an average score of 4.23 on the prompt "Fosters an atmosphere of collaboration among team members," compared to a 3.58 average for less-effective leaders. The message is clear: Less-effective leaders of virtual teams find it especially difficult to build relationships and develop collaboration among team members.

Moldenhauer-Salazar believes, "The lack of face-to-face contact makes building trust very difficult. Leaders need to reinforce the message that people can rely on one another. When virtual team leaders become the 'hub' of all communication, it causes problems which likely stem from a lack of trust."

Effective leaders of virtual teams help build an environment that supports collaboration by finding ways for team members to interact and communicate informally. For example, "same-time" technologies like instant messaging will help increase more spontaneous communication.

Another important component of promoting collaboration is productively managing the conflicts that emerge. Top-performing virtual team leaders score a 4.03 on their ability to handle conflict effectively, while low-performing team leaders scored a 3.39. Because conflict can often initially go undetected in virtual environments, leaders must proactively look for signs of it and take steps to resolve it in a timely manner.

Following are a few tips on how leaders can build trust and manage conflict to enhance collaboration in a virtual environment:

- Acknowledge and respect cultural differences related to communication and recognition norms.
- Identify ways to stay in touch with team members and determine which methods are most effective with specific individuals.
- Reinforce shared team goals and the role each team member plays in the successful achievement of those goals
- Clarify performance expectations so everyone knows what to expect from the other members of the team
- For critical team activities and decisions, clarify when cooperation is necessary; agree on who needs to be involved and the level of each person's authority
- Ensure that virtual team members are comfortable giving feedback virtually; teach and model good communication and conflict management skills.
- Encourage participation and reinforce an environment of constructive debate.
- Keep in mind that "trust" can mean different things to different generations, cultures, and individuals. Focus on moving from task-based trust to interpersonal trust by communicating openly and honestly, leading by example, employing consistent team interactions, and being accessible and responsive.
- Deal with conflicts quickly so they don't fester over time.

- To keep problems from becoming personal, focus on the problem not the person.
- "Stand in the other person's shoes" and try to see the issue from all sides.
- When situations escalate, return to the facts of the problem and avoid personal issues.
- Periodically check in with team members who may otherwise begin to feel isolated and believe they lack support.
- Create a shared virtual space for informal team communication.

Differentiator 3: Ability to Communicate Team Goals and Direction

Successful leaders of virtual teams clearly articulate team goals and direction to ensure that everyone has a shared target. They also periodically revisit these factors both to reinforce their importance and to make adjustments as necessary.

Top-performing leaders in our study were more effective than low-performing team leaders at communicating team goals (average score of 4.12 compared to 3.48, respectively).

Clearly communicated, shared team goals are especially crucial for virtual teams because they give members a sense of purpose and meaning that sustains them when they are working alone or without regular direct contact with the team leader or other team members. Clear goals also help to unify the actions of a geographically dispersed team and keep members focused on execution.

Effective virtual leaders also communicate how their teams' goals align with the broader organizational strategy so members know in no uncertain terms how their work impacts the organization. Here are some tips for developing and communicating virtual team goals:

- Early on in a team's formation, provide a clear sense of purpose. Explain how the team's work contributes to the organization's overall goals and revisit these goals as things progress.

- Invite key stakeholders to v-meetings to discuss how the team's work impacts the organizational strategy.

- Involve team members in discussions about setting or prioritizing goals to increase commitment.

- Ensure that the virtual team's goals are mutually supportive of other functions and teams.

- Periodically revisit goals to ensure that, given changes in the internal or external environment, they are still appropriate and feasible.

- Put a process in place to set and reset priorities; frequently revisit priorities and recalibrate as necessary.

- To be effective, goal statements must be SMART:

  - *Specific:* The goal should be expressed in terms of a specific outcome or result for which the team will be held accountable. This outcome should be linked to a specific business objective.

  - *Measurable:* The goal should be expressed in terms of an outcome that can be measured or otherwise verified.

  - *Aligned:* The goal should be challenging but realistic given the current environment, available resources, and the team's experience and skill level.

  - *Realistic:* The goal should be consistent with the organization's/team's strategic objectives.

  - *Time-bound:* The goal should include a target date or deadline by which it will be met.

Differentiator 4: Strong Interpersonal Communication Skills

It's no secret that team members who work virtually sometimes feel isolated and find it more difficult to tap into the office grapevine. This feeling of isolation can negatively impact morale and productivity. Therefore, the most effective leaders establish informal and formal communication methods to ensure that people have the information they need to do their jobs and to feel "plugged in" and engaged.

Moldenhauer-Salazar, who emphasizes the importance of effective communication for virtual team leaders, said, "I think they have to be over-communicators and also very good communicators. They have to make sure that their messages were heard. They know how to match the technology to the task. For example, email communications should be clear and succinct."

When we interviewed team members and stakeholders, they consistently mentioned responsiveness and follow-up as critical elements of communication. Our study also found that top-performing virtual team leaders had higher ratings on several items related to communication effectiveness. For example, they scored significantly higher on responding effectively, providing timely feedback to team members, and sharing information in a timely manner.

Despite the lack of regular face-to-face time, effective virtual team leaders create a two-way dialogue so members feel comfortable giving constructive feedback. Doing this over the phone, a primary communication option for virtual teams, is particularly challenging because members have no visual cues to gauge the reactions of others. That's why effective leaders learn to choose their words wisely and to use a more neutral tone of voice when asking for and responding to feedback.

To determine your own communication skills strengths and weaknesses, participate in the self-assessment in Exhibit 5.2. Then use the tips included here to outline steps you can take to enhance your skills.

Exhibit 5.2. Self-Assessment: Interpersonal Communication Skills

Part I

Using the scale provided, rate yourself on each of the following items:

1 = Never	2 = Sometimes	3 = Almost All of the Time

Item	Rating
1. I clearly communicate and explain what I need/expect from others and why.	
2. I consider the impact of my message on the receiver(s).	
3. I help people maintain a positive self-image. I avoid statements or actions that make people "lose face."	
4. I listen effectively to others (even if I don't like what I'm hearing, disagree, or am extremely busy).	
5. I restate what others say in my own words to show that I heard their ideas.	
6. I restate others' feelings to show empathy.	
7. I ask open-ended questions to gather information and to clarify information.	
8. I provide helpful feedback on others' performance and ideas.	
9. I ask others for feedback on my performance and ideas.	
10. I welcome feedback rather than becoming defensive.	
11. I think through what I'm going to say and how to say it.	
12. I plan a communication strategy to accomplish my goals.	

Part II

Based on your assessment of the items in Part I, identify two or three of your major communication strengths:

Identify two or three things you want to focus on (do more frequently or more effectively) to develop your communication skills.

What two or three things can you do to improve your communication skills? Be sure to revisit this once you finish reading the chapter.

Following are a few tips to help improve your communication skills when leading from a distance:

- Ask others for feedback on your listening and communication skills. Ask them what works well and what you can do differently to put your ideas across more effectively.
- Identify the best way to share information with virtual team members. For example, what situations are more appropriate for phone calls, emails, etc.?
- Provide team members with status reports on upcoming changes.
- Confirm important communications, such as a complex new assignment or key policies, in writing.
- Present an overview of your team's activities, capabilities, and achievements to upper-level management.
- Before you send a report, email, or memo, ask yourself:
  - Is the purpose clear and up-front?
  - Have I avoided unnecessary words?

- ○ Do my ideas flow smoothly and logically?
- ○ Did I use bullets and subheadings for visual appeal?
- ○ Is each step clearly communicated?

- Participate in a writing skills workshop, review a self-study audiotape or video on effective writing, or talk with someone you regard as an excellent writer to ask for tips.

- For each message ask:
  - ○ What is the overall purpose or main idea I want to communicate?
  - ○ Why is it important to communicate it?
  - ○ To whom will I communicate it?
  - ○ How will I communicate it (face-to-face, in writing, an email, at a meeting)?
  - ○ What impact is the message likely to have on the receiver(s)?
  - ○ How will I respond to the receiver's anticipated reaction to the message?

- Ensure two-way communication. First, listen to make sure you heard what the other person said, then paraphrase what was said to show others that they have been heard and understood. This helps reduce defensiveness, promotes self-esteem, and defuses emotional exchanges, which, in turn, enables people to engage in productive problem solving.

- Actively listen when people come to you with a concern, a question, or an idea.

- Ensure that you are comfortable giving feedback to team members virtually.

- Model the behavior you want from others.

- Provide team members with a framework for giving effective feedback.

Differentiator 5: Ability to Empower Team Members

A research study discussed in the *Academy of Management Journal*[7] investigated the role of empowerment on virtual team performance. The study found that, in virtual teams, empowerment was significantly connected to process improvement and customer satisfaction. Because people are often expected to work more independently in virtual teams, finding ways to delegate work, to give team members freedom to make decisions, and to monitor work become particularly important for success.

While delegating work and checking on the progress of work are important facets of empowerment, they're more difficult in a virtual setting. Top-performing leaders in our study were more effective at delegating responsibilities than less-effective leaders were (average score of 4.0 to 3.5, respectively). They also encouraged team members to come up with creative ideas more consistently (average score of 4.21 compared to 3.71), which is another way to motivate team members and encourage process improvement.

Once they delegate assignments, monitoring progress can be difficult for virtual team leaders. The best leaders set up processes for monitoring progress and follow up, but avoid micromanaging their members.

According to Kevin Squires, director of payroll administration at Saint-Gobain, "Successful virtual team leaders manage the balance between independence and micromanagement. They also take steps to engage people who may feel isolated."

Monitoring makes it possible to identify potential problems early on, prevents disruptions in team activities and service to customers, and ensures that people are held accountable for the quality of their work. This information is then used to formulate and modify team objectives, strategies, policies, and procedures.

In addition, monitoring provides the information needed to solve problems and make decisions effectively, to evaluate team members' performance, to recognize achievements, to identify performance deficiencies, to assess training needs, to provide assistance, and to allocate rewards such as pay increases or promotions.

The appropriate degree of monitoring required depends on the specifics of the situation, for example, the kind of work being performed and level of experience of the team members. Naturally, monitoring is more important when virtual team members are inexperienced or apathetic about the work. Likewise, it's essential when mistakes or delays will significantly impact the success of the project and have to be quickly remedied.

So, given the lack of face-to-face contact, how do effective virtual team leaders monitor their team members' work? A common method for monitoring progress on assignments and projects is to obtain update or status reports from team members based on the tasks they've been given. The type of information and level of detail in progress reports should be agreed on when a new project is initiated or a new assignment is made.

However, in lieu of status reports, many team leaders choose to frequently follow up with individual team members to ensure they're on track. This proactive approach can be more effective when managing remote teams, but to avoid the perception of micromanaging, team leaders should determine the frequency of these check-ins with each team member.

Some virtual teams use online support tools to track projects and initiatives, which allows the leader to assess progress in a non-intrusive manner. Establishing clear reporting requirements in advance is also an effective approach, and it helps leaders avoid monitoring too closely and communicating a lack of trust.

Most importantly, the success of monitoring depends on obtaining accurate information from people who may be reluctant to provide it. For example, team members may be hesitant to inform their team leaders about problems, mistakes, and delays. People who aren't responsible for a problem may be reluctant to report it if they are concerned about becoming the target of an angry outburst—otherwise known as "kill-the-messenger" syndrome.

Therefore, it's essential that the reaction to problems be constructive and non-punitive. Questions should be open-ended and non-evaluative to encourage people to respond and provide a more complete picture of the situation. Questions should be phrased so as to communicate the leader's concerns and expectations to team members, in addition to seeking to obtain information. To determine your own empowerment strengths and opportunity areas, complete the self-assessment in Exhibit 5.3.

Exhibit 5.3. Self-Assessment: Empowering Others

Use this assessment to help you evaluate your effectiveness at delegating and empowering others. Read each item and, using the rating scale provided, rate the extent to which each item describes your behavior.

1 = Never	2 = Sometimes	3 = Almost All of the Time

Item	Rating
1. I consider the skills of my team (their competence level) when delegating tasks.	
2. I give team members a variety of challenging assignments that will strengthen or develop their abilities.	
3. I ask team members to represent me in meetings/events as developmental opportunities.	
4. I generally delegate work, even though it may be faster/easier to do it myself.	
5. When delegating, I provide time for people to ask questions.	
6. I provide specific feedback about an individual's performance on a delegated project.	
7. I delegate tasks but follow up to make sure that team members have the resources/information needed to be successful.	
8. When delegating, I provide the big picture and the relevant facts needed to achieve the desired outcome.	

Item	Rating
9. After delegating something, I check in periodically but avoid "micromanagement."	
10. I delegate parts of a project when I cannot delegate the whole thing.	
11. I encourage team members to make autonomous decisions when appropriate.	
12. I encourage team members to generate creative solutions to solve problems.	

Obstacles at a Glance: A Quick Reference Guide

Virtual teams frequently face common obstacles that impede their performance. We've outlined these in the following Quick Reference Guide (Table 5.2) to allow leaders to diagnose a team's problems and view several recommended solutions.

Table 5.2 Leader Quick Reference Guide

Problem	Solutions
Team members are not collaborating effectively to achieve team goals.	• Identify what deliverables the team needs to collaborate on and come up with a plan to ensure that team members are working on things jointly. • Clarify roles and levels of authority so team members know what to expect from each other. • Assess what barriers are preventing communication and collaboration. • Once a plan is in place, set milestones to periodically assess performance.

(continued overleaf)

Table 5.2 (*Continued*)

Problem	Solutions
Team members do not trust one another.	• Take time to assess what factors are leading to a lack of trust. Is there a problem between certain team members or subgroups?
	• If appropriate, have a candid discussion with individual team members or as a group to discuss how the team will move forward.
	• Confirm that goals and roles are clear and agreed on. Lack of trust can result when people are working at cross purposes and mistakenly appear to not be supporting each other.
	• Ensure that virtual team members have time to build relationships with one another.
Team members are not meetings goals/objectives.	• Take time to diagnose the problem to see what is getting in the way of effective execution.
	• Consider the following: – Does the team have clear goals with due dates and assigned responsibilities? – Do team members have clear roles? – Are sufficient resources available? – Do people have too many commitments? – Is everything Priority 1? – Are team members being held accountable? If not, put a plan in place to monitor the work. – When people do not deliver on commitments, follow up with them to understand why. – As priorities change, ensure that everyone knows what to focus on.
The team does not handle conflict appropriately.	• When a conflict occurs, clarify the situation by identifying the individuals involved in the conflict, defining the issues in question, and gathering facts and perceptions of the people involved.

Table 5.2 (*Continued*)

Problem	*Solutions*
	• Use a seven-step process for managing conflict:
	1. Describe what's important to you and why it is important.
	2. Make sure you understand what's important to the other person and why it is important.
	3. Identify common ground and look for points of interdependence.
	4. Invite alternatives that address your needs/goals and the other person's needs/goals.
	5. Use active listening (paraphrase and repeat what you are told, ask open-ended questions, give balanced responses) to evaluate alternatives, resolve concerns, and improve ideas.
	6. If an alternative isn't immediately available, temporarily remove constraints to invite and propose new alternatives.
	7. End the discussion by summarizing key points and stating next steps.
Team performance seems to be stagnant.	• Assess the objectives of the team to determine whether it still serves an important purpose. (We often see cases where team members have been together for several years but no longer have common objectives.)
	• People often lose interest in the team's work, particularly when teams have been together for a long period of time. Reinforce the sense of purpose by reminding people how their work contributes to the "big picture."

(*continued overleaf*)

Table 5.2 (*Continued*)

Problem	Solutions
	• Look for opportunities to expand or change the responsibilities of team members to engage them more. Rotating different roles might be a solution. For example, assign a different meeting facilitator for each meeting.
	• Have an internal or external customer discuss how the work of the team impacts his or her group.
Team members may feel isolated.	• Actively seek out participation from these team members by asking them to share their ideas during v-meetings or by having them take the lead on a given task. Track participation on calls to make sure that everyone is involved.
	• Partner several of the isolated team members together on a project.

Conclusion

The challenges virtual team leaders face are often exacerbated by their virtual setting. However, the most effective leaders are able to implement strategies that help address these performance barriers.

We've pinpointed five leadership differentiators—top-performing virtual team leaders are able to successfully manage change, foster collaboration, communicate team goals and direction, use strong interpersonal communication skills, and empower team members. While these skills may seem fundamental, many of the virtual team leaders in our study were not able to execute them effectively.

Understanding that leading from a distance can be more challenging than leading co-located teams is the first step in addressing the problems that virtual team leaders face. Therefore, it is important for organizations to provide necessary skill training for virtual team leaders and to periodically assess their performance.

The Bottom Line

The most effective virtual team leaders use strategies to balance the execution-oriented factors with the interpersonal and communication factors that are critical for virtual team success.

Chapter Six

What Factors Really Accelerate Virtual Team Performance—The Four Top Performance Boosters

> "Coming together is a beginning. Keeping together is progress. Working together is success."
>
> —*Henry Ford*

> "It's easy to get good players. Getting them to play together, that's the hard part."
>
> —*Casey Stengel*

Is your virtual team performing effectively? If your answer is no, take heart. There *are* steps you can take to improve performance.

In the previous chapter we focused on the factors that separate the best virtual team leaders from the rest of the pack. Now we'll explore what team leaders can do to help their teams overcome performance challenges.

Our study found that there are four main practices that virtual team leaders can use to boost their teams' performance levels: provide coaching and support, gain the commitment of team members, recognize the contributions of team members, and hold team members accountable. Read on to learn more about each one.

Taking Virtual Team Performance to the Next Level

Performance Booster 1: Provide Coaching and Support

To ensure each team member maximizes his or her contributions, virtual team leaders need to consistently monitor progress and provide frequent feedback and coaching. Doing so helps team members link their day-to-day activities and behaviors with their teams' overall goals.

Our study found that top-performing leaders were more effective at coaching team members than were less-effective leaders (average score of 4.04 compared to 3.24, respectively). However, the study also found that virtual team leaders often believe they provide more coaching and support than they actually do.

When we compared team member and team leader perceptions of the leader's effectiveness, we found that leaders had an inflated view of their coaching skills. Specifically, there was a gap of approximately .50 between leader and team member ratings—the biggest gap across all team leader survey items.

Ongoing coaching and feedback are most effective when provided through frequent one-on-one interactions. There are two types of coaching situations. One is on-the-spot coaching. This method helps leaders reinforce positive behaviors, adjust negative behaviors before they lead to serious problems, or get poor performing team members back on track.

Obviously, on-the-spot coaching can be difficult when you are unable to have spontaneous, face-to-face interactions with a team member. This makes it even more important to ensure you have regular points of contact with your team members and to establish a good relationship with them so that, when you do need to provide feedback virtually, they will be more receptive.

The second situation involves using coaching to monitor progress toward reaching goals. Here coaching focuses on overall performance, including results, activities, and behaviors. This coaching method allows leaders to take a broader view so they can assess whether goals are appropriate, what obstacles may be preventing their achievement, and what team members can do in the long term to enhance their own performance and that of the team as whole.

This type of coaching requires detailed knowledge about each team member. Why? Because leaders will need to assess how well a given team member is performing relative to expectations.

As with on-the-spot coaching, in order to have sufficient concrete data about a given team member's performance, virtual team leaders must establish processes that facilitate regular contact and communication. Otherwise, the coaching interaction will either be too general to be helpful or off target and inaccurate, which can cause defensiveness and squelch motivation.

It may help to view the interaction between the team leader and team members as a continuum that stretches between a *directing* and a *coaching* style, as shown in Table 6.1. Virtual team leaders who use a directing style tend to be authoritative and use one-way communication with team members. On the other hand, leaders who demonstrate a coaching style are often described as being collaborative, engaging, supportive, and inclusive. Effective leaders are able to decide where on this continuum they must operate and under what conditions.

Coaching is quite different from directing. A coach does not always give the "right" answer to a problem. In fact, he or she may not even know the "right" answer, and doesn't try to hide that fact. Instead, he or she serves more as a sounding board for a person's ideas, a supportive critic (when necessary) of those ideas, a source of facts and ideas derived from a broader experience base, and sometimes a devil's advocate to test the strength of plans before they're formally implemented. The most effective virtual

Table 6.1 Virtual Leadership Continuum

Directing	Coaching
Competes	Collaborates
Is directive	Is development-oriented
Reinforces authority	Reinforces networking
Holds back information	Shares information
Encourages dependency	Encourages self-management
Dictates	Problem solves
Allows less autonomy	Allows more autonomy

very simplistic generalization

unfair comparison

team leaders are coaches, who listen, ask, facilitate, integrate, and provide support.

Let's take a look at two virtual team leaders from our interviews. The first is Dan. He was the leader of a global virtual team in a manufacturing company. He was very direct when assigning tasks and did not consider team members' expertise or interests. He failed to check on the progress of work and would frequently find out that people couldn't meet deadlines or had experienced unexpected obstacles. And on occasion, during team v-meetings, Dan would chastise certain team members while the rest of the team was still on the call.

Stephanie is the second leader. She led a global team in an insurance company. She set clear goals for the team and—in contrast to Dan—put standard processes in place for checking on the team's progress. She delegated work based on her team members' skills and interests and then allowed people to work autonomously.

Stephanie also consulted team members when problems arose and created a collaborative atmosphere where people shared ideas and helped one another address issues. She recognized individual team member accomplishments in front of the whole team and also provided rewards to the team and individual members.

Not surprisingly, Stephanie's team members felt she was an effective leader, and her team was very successful. Dan, however, received negative feedback from team members and stakeholders, and his team struggled with performance issues.

What's the bottom line? Based on our research and experience working with virtual teams, the most successful leaders use more of a coaching style to engage and motivate team members, rather than being overly directive, which tends to be less effective.

Here are a few tips that will help you become a better coach for your virtual team members:

- Identify, discuss, and set next steps for what each team member could do to develop knowledge, skills, and abilities to maximize his or her potential and make an even greater contribution to the team.

- Monitor the progress team members are making toward achieving their goals.

- Delegate tasks and work assignments that are consistent with team members' current capabilities and support their development goals.

- Provide constructive criticism to improve performance by citing specific examples of what the person did and did not do versus your expectations in specific situations and by describing the impact of his or her behavior.

- Ask for team member ideas for improving performance. Be ready to offer feedback (but don't lecture!). Agree on next steps for improvement and a time for a follow-up conversation.

- Look for opportunities to be a mentor. Think about your strengths and the special knowledge, skills, and experience you have that could benefit others. Consider what you would enjoy helping others learn and what you would hope to gain from a mentoring relationship.

- Take time to learn about the career goals of team members and about where they would like to be in the future.

- Emphasize each individual's responsibility for managing his or her own career and discuss what you could do to support his or her efforts.

- Challenge people to do new things, to explore, to reach their potential. Be willing and ready to push them toward achieving their goals.

Performance Booster 2: Gain Team Members' Commitment

Leading a team means you have to encourage people to carry out requests, support proposals, and implement decisions. The most successful virtual team leaders know the level of support they need doesn't happen automatically. It must be cultivated. Therefore, these leaders take time to get buy-in from team members for plans, tasks, and initiatives.

In our study, top-performing team leaders were more effective at obtaining team members' support than less successful virtual team leaders (average scores of 4.2 compared with 3.51, respectively). Our research indicates that there are four "core tactics" that are most effective for gaining team member buy-in. They are *rational persuasion, inspirational appeals, consultation,* and *collaboration*. Let's take a closer look at each of them.

Rational Persuasion.   Rational persuasion involves the use of explanations, logical arguments, and factual evidence to explain why a request or proposal will benefit the organization or help achieve an important objective. This tactic may also involve presenting factual evidence that shows how and why a project or change is likely to be successful. Rational persuasion is a flexible tactic that can be effective when you are trying to influence either your direct reports, your boss, or your peers. Rational persuasion is most effective when the person you are trying to persuade shares your task objectives but does not recognize that your proposal is the best way to attain those objectives. Specific guidelines include:

- Explain the reason for a request or proposal.
- Provide evidence that your proposal is feasible.
- Explain why your proposal is better than competing ones.
- Explain how likely problems or concerns would be handled.

During our study, we observed a case when rational persuasion was used effectively. Tom, a virtual team leader, needed his team members to commit to implementing a major change within their IT process. Prior to the meeting, Tom sent out information about the problems that existed with the current process, as well as several proposed ideas for a new approach. During the call, he discussed the rationale and business case for the change by providing data that reinforced the need. In addition, he conducted a discussion with team members about the tradeoffs of each proposal and any implications for the team.

While there was initial resistance, Tom's ability to provide meaningful data helped team members move from resistance to approval.

Inspirational Appeals. In contrast to the logical arguments used in rational persuasion, this tactic involves an emotional or value-based appeal. An inspirational appeal is an attempt to develop enthusiasm and commitment by arousing strong emotions and linking a request or proposal to a person's needs, values, hopes, and ideals. Top-performing virtual team leaders in our study scored higher on inspiring people compared with less-effective team leaders (average score of 4.08 compared to 3.48, respectively). Specific guidelines include:

- Appeal to the person's ideals and values.
- Link the request to the person's self-image.
- Link the request to a clear and appealing vision.
- Use a dramatic, expressive style of speaking.
- Use positive, optimistic language.

Let's take a look at a virtual team leader, Matt, who used inspirational appeals to gain buy-in from his team. Matt was asked to lead a global task force of talented individuals to develop recommendations to address a competitive product offering. The team members were all busy executives who would need to dedicate a significant amount of time to the team in addition to the time they spent completing day-to-day roles and responsibilities. None of them reported to Matt, and he needed to ensure that people were motivated to do the work.

Matt conducted a virtual kick-off meeting during which he invited senior executives from the company to discuss the importance of the team's objective. These leaders emphasized how the team's contributions would impact the company's bottom line and lead to greater customer satisfaction. They also spent time outlining the talent and prior business achievements of each team member—a great way to recognize people for their quality work and help team members get to know one another.

These techniques inspired the team. They wanted to add value to the organization, and after much hard work, the team was very successful.

Consultation. This tactic centers on inviting the other person to participate in planning how to carry out a request or implement a proposed change. Not surprisingly, top-performing virtual team leaders in our research were more effective at seeking input from team members than less successful team leaders (average score of 4.12 compared with 3.55, respectively).

Consultation can take a variety of forms that involve different degrees of participation. The least amount of involvement occurs when you present a detailed proposal or plan and ask the person to provide feedback. After hearing his or concerns, questions, and so forth, you can either explain why they are unwarranted or modify the proposal to deal with them.

A greater degree of involvement occurs when you present a general strategy or objective, rather than a detailed proposal, and ask the person to suggest specific action steps for implementing it. The suggested action steps are then discussed until there is agreement by both parties. Specific guidelines include:

- State your objective and ask what the person can do to help.
- Ask for suggestions on how to improve a tentative proposal.
- Involve the person in planning how to attain an objective.
- Respond to the person's concerns and suggestions.

Team leader Tom also serves as a good example of how to effectively use consultation. When evaluating alternatives to his IT change, Tom was sure to include team members. He also solicited their feedback on how to deal with potential problems. And he listened to team members' concerns and addressed them in a positive manner.

What do you think would have happened if Tom had simply informed team members that a change was being implemented and told them they'd better get on board? Chances are he would have encountered a great deal of resistance. By involving team members in the process up-front, he was able to effectively deal with any concerns and gain people's commitment for the change.

Of course, there is a downside to consultation. Sometimes when you ask for others' input you will receive suggestions that may not be relevant or feasible. In these situations, we recommend using a technique called the *balanced response*, which allows you to provide constructive feedback without being confrontational or diminishing self-esteem.

The balanced response identifies the "pluses" of the feedback and addresses concerns about the person's ideas or performance in a positive, constructive way. A balanced response has two parts. First, state what you like about the person's idea, suggestion, or performance—the positives. Second, state what you see as the key concerns or what, in your opinion, keeps the person's idea or performance from being totally acceptable. Here are a few sample lead-ins for presenting positives:

- "What I like about your idea/performance is...."
- "The benefits are...."
- "The strengths are...."
- "What I found especially helpful was...."

Here are a few lead-ins for expressing concerns:

- "How can we...?"
- "What I'm concerned about is...."

- "Some things that might be improved on are...."
- "I wish we could...."

Table 6.2 summarizes the ways to use this technique.

Collaboration. This influence tactic involves an offer to provide the necessary resources and/or assistance if the person will carry out a request or approve a proposal. Collaboration involves reducing the difficulty or costs of carrying out a request, and it's especially appropriate when compliance will be difficult for the other person. It usually involves a joint effort to accomplish the task. In our study, high-performing virtual team leaders helped team members achieve goals much more frequently than less-effective virtual team leaders did (average score of 4.11 compared with 3.41, respectively). Specific guidelines include:

- Offer to provide necessary assistance or resources.
- Offer to help the person solve problems caused by a request.
- Offer to help the person implement a proposed change.

Let's look at an example of collaboration from our study. Jennifer was the leader of a large human resources team and

Table 6.2 Balanced Response "Do's" and "Don'ts"

Do...	Don't...
• Start with the positives. • Identify concerns. • Invite ways to overcome concerns by asking open-ended questions (e.g., "How can we...?").	• Invite suggestions unless you are willing to consider them. • Say, "But..." after discussing positives. • Start by focusing on the negatives. • Use the words, "Always," "Never," and "Should" when coaching.

effectively used collaboration to gain commitment from team members. This team had been working on multiple high-priority projects, and many team members had been working long hours. Jennifer's manager, the senior vice president of human resources, called Jennifer and told her that the head of sales had an urgent request that Jennifer's team would need to handle.

Jennifer knew that her team members were already over-whelmed. However, she also knew that this project was of critical importance. Rather than simply asking her team to add on another project, Jennifer called a virtual meeting and explained the request. She asked for team members' input on how to prioritize all of their projects and solicited their input about what resources would be necessary to meet all existing commitments. Jennifer proposed several options that would free up resources and offered to take on some of the work herself.

By getting everything out on the table in the beginning, Jennifer and her team were able to openly discuss what they would need to do performance-wise and what resources they would need to reach their goals—rather than allowing team member complaints and problems to fester as the project got underway.

Performance Booster 3: Recognize Team Members' Contributions

Many leaders believe it's difficult to recognize virtual teams and their individual team members. After all, it's not always easy to determine which team members are contributing what. Or if they do know who should be recognized, they have trouble coming up with meaningful ways to do so for team members they don't see face-to-face. Yet, the highly effective virtual team leaders in our study make sure they find ways to do so.

Moldenhauer-Salazar believes that public acknowledgement is important to inspire and recognize people. "When people are there in person, it is beneficial to acknowledge people and the team as a whole," says Moldenhauer-Salazar. "I have seen a lot of managers defer to spot bonuses for virtual teams because they don't come up with alternative reward strategies. I do think these things are appreciated, particularly if they are personal."

Although recognition does not take up much of a leader's time, providing it is one of the most powerful and underused techniques for motivating, rewarding, and retaining good people. And keep in mind that, although recognition requires more ingenuity than money, recognition is not limited by budget.

Some of the most effective forms of recognition are quite simple. Setting up a recognition system that inspires team members and rewards success need not be time-consuming or costly.

For example, we recently worked with a virtual team leader who periodically sends e-cards, e-certificates and references accomplishments in a team newsletter. In another example, a team leader has celebrated successes and recognized team members who have made special contributions by e-mailing the entire team about them.

Sahota, who leads a large virtual organization, says that the company's Shining Performance virtual recognition program allows leaders to recognize others. The program has different levels, ranging from e-certificates to monetary rewards. And, when possible, Sahota also brings teams together in person to celebrate their achievements.

If a high-performing team member is not actually a direct report to the team's leader, effective virtual leaders make it a practice to inform that team member's direct manager and other stakeholders about his or her accomplishments.

In our experience, there are several important factors to keep in mind when recognizing others:

- Offer recognition frequently.
- Provide recognition in a timely manner.
- Be sincere.

- Reference a specific example of the desired behavior.
- Do not mix messages by recognizing while trying to correct performance.
- Recognize only those employees who have performed the desired behavior.
- Tell others—team members, stakeholders, other leaders—about the person's good performance.
- Be sure to communicate praise that you've heard from others to the appropriate person.
- Make an effort to avoid habitually following recognition with a request or other constructive feedback. Let the praise stand alone.
- Use recognition to bring out and reinforce the best in others.
- Find out what kinds of recognition team members value the most. Don't assume that they value the same things you value or that money is the only form of recognition that works. Be creative in identifying and providing recognition that meets individual and group needs.
- Look for opportunities to provide recognition for a job well done. Be specific by using the "What? So What?" model. Try to "catch" someone doing something right every day.

Here are some ways to recognize virtual teams and team members:

- Use virtual ceremonies or special events to celebrate individual and team accomplishments.
- Recognize their accomplishments in a company newsletter, on a recognition bulletin board, or on the team intranet or website.
- Provide food—order lunch or breakfast for team members in different locations.

- Identify challenging assignments that use their strengths.
- Provide increased autonomy and authority to make decisions.
- Offer the opportunity to attend training on a topic of interest.
- Take the person out for lunch or dinner when you are visiting in person.
- Provide e-certificates of recognition.
- Provide tickets to a sporting event or show.
- Provide a gift certificate (or e-gift card).

While there are numerous strategies that virtual team leaders can use to recognize their teams, the most effective leaders take steps to match the form of recognition to the team member's individual needs and motives.

Performance Booster 4: Hold Team Members Accountable

Virtual team leaders often struggle with holding team members accountable for their actions. Bruce Fern and Herb Cohen, of Performance Connections International, identified four common accountability mistakes that leaders make—mistakes that were each supported by our interviews with team leaders.[1]

> *Mistake 1. Not clearly communicating who will be held accountable for what.* During conference calls, to establish accountability, effective team leaders ensure that each commitment is tied to a specific person (or group of people) and that that person or group of people understands their responsibilities.
>
> *Mistake 2. Agreeing on an action, but without any discussion of a completion date.* As a result the end date is open to interpretation and—not surprisingly—tasks are not completed on time.

Mistake 3. Waiting until the completion date to check on results, or not even checking in at all. Many virtual team leaders are hesitant to monitor progress because they are concerned that checking in too frequently will annoy team members and will be perceived as micromanaging. As a result, they often learn about missed deadlines or delays when it is too late to make other arrangements.

Mistake 4. Not holding people accountable for missed commitments after the fact. Even though many virtual team leaders would rather ignore performance problems, doing so has negative consequences. First, it creates a tone that it is acceptable to miss set deadlines. Second, when performance problems are not addressed, they are more likely to keep occurring. And keep in mind that if a leader waits to address a problem, it becomes even more difficult because previous situations were ignored.

Finally, some of the barriers to execution that led to the missed deadline or commitment are likely to remain in place. Having a discussion about problems and obstacles that impeded performance helps prevent the same issues from popping up in the future.

Three techniques virtual team leaders can use to avoid these four mistakes are discussed below. Just as air traffic controllers must juggle different flights simultaneously to make sure every plane takes off and lands safely, you must help your direct reports, peers, and even your manager, juggle their priorities to ensure every commitment they make begins and ends smoothly and successfully.

The best way to manage accountability is to ensure team members follow through in the first place. The acronym ATC (air traffic control) can help you remember these techniques.[2]

- *Action.* Regardless of how good a team member's idea is or how sincere his or her intention is, nothing can happen until a team member commits to taking action. Actions must be stated in behavioral language. Who specifically will do what?

- *Timetable*. Defines who will do what by when. Commitments that don't have a time frame usually fall by the wayside.

- *Checkpoints*. Set up specific progress checks on the path to the completion date. Do not wait until the completion date itself to check on progress.

Most leaders don't use this last technique because they don't want to ask a question that might make it sound like they have doubts about a team member's performance, saying, for example, "Did you conduct those coaching sessions the way you said you would?" Asking the question in this way *is* ineffective because it communicates the assumption that the action was not done.

Leaders should instead phrase the question so that it communicates the assumption that the action was completed, for example, "How are the coaching sessions going?" "How did your manager react to the resource request?" or "Have you been having any trouble collecting that information?"

If you learn that the action has not been completed or there has not been any progress, in a non-punitive manner ask what the person will do to get things on track or ask how you can help the person get things back on track.

There are also two strategies you can use to increase accountability if someone has dropped the ball. (But remember, prevention is always better than an after-the-fact remedy!)[3]

Ask Three Accountability Questions. Coach the other person to ask him- or herself these questions non-defensively:

- *Past*: "What could I have done to prevent the problem? What, if anything, did I do that might possibly have contributed to the problem?"

- *Present:* "What can I do NOW to get on track?"
- *Future:* "What can I do to prevent this problem from happening again in the future?"

Be Aware of the Possibility of a Defensive Response and Reduce It. Help the person be aware when he or she is being defensive. Don't blame the person for being defensive (If you do, he or she will only become more defensive), but gently point it out. Help the person recognize when he or she is giving a defensive response:

- After she has become defensive, help her acknowledge it.
- During a defensive response, help him be aware of it.
- Use the "24-Hour Rule"—come back to it later if necessary.

By following the tips and guidelines that characterize top-performing virtual team leaders, you can enhance your ability to lead from a distance. As organizations continue to expand the use of virtual teams, team leadership will play an increasingly important role in driving the effectiveness of these teams.

Organizations should select virtual team leaders who are able to apply the key characteristics required for effectively managing from a distance. In addition, they should periodically assess virtual team leader effectiveness to provide targeted feedback about how they can improve their performance.

Virtual team leaders are the leaders of the future . . . invest in them and you'll reap the performance benefits for years to come.

Conclusion

Virtual team leaders need to be diligent about how they coach, recognize, influence, and hold team members accountable for meeting commitments. These skills are important for improving the effectiveness of virtual teams.

Many of these skills are challenging for leaders of co-located teams and can be even more difficult when leading from a distance. However, the good news is that virtual team leaders who use these proven strategies will enhance the effectiveness of their teams.

The Bottom Line

Although certain resources such as technology may be viewed as the foundation for virtual team effectiveness, the role team leaders play is too often overlooked. The reality is that great virtual team leaders are crucial for success.

Chapter Seven

How to Facilitate High-Impact Virtual Meetings—Techniques That Really Work

"The art of communication is the language of leadership."

—James Humes

We frequently encounter virtual team leaders who *think* they are effective. However, when it's time to bring everyone together and really "get stuff done" they struggle to effectively communicate with and engage their team members. That's right. One of the biggest trouble spots for leaders is the virtual team meeting.

We hear stories all the time about marathon v-meetings—some even lasting all day—that quickly lose focus and end up being a waste of everyone's time. We also often hear about regularly scheduled v-meetings that are conducted without clear objectives and agendas, but that continue simply because they are on everyone's calendar.

As we've touched on in earlier chapters, virtual team members are time-crunched and often spread quite thin between their day-to-day responsibilities and their virtual team responsibilities. Poorly run meetings not only waste their already scarce time, but they can also jeopardize the team's ability to meet its deadlines.

These factors are why many of the executives we interviewed reinforced the importance of knowing how to effectively manage virtual meetings. For example, Theresa Zeller of Merck stated, "Managing work/life balance is a huge challenge. You need to be flexible but also do not want to reinforce working 24/7, as you want to be respectful of setting virtual boundaries. Therefore, it is important to have much better practices in terms of meeting etiquette and managing meetings."

Given that successful virtual meetings are essential, in this chapter we offer up a few practical strategies and tools to help virtual team leaders and meeting facilitators better manage v-meetings, advance their quality, and improve the results they produce.

The Facilitator's Role

The virtual meeting facilitator, regardless of whether the person filling the role is the team leader or a team member, plays a crucial role in making v-meetings a worthwhile experience. He or she guides the process, encourages suggestions, keeps the team on track, summarizes actions, creates a positive climate, and anticipates pitfalls.

Great facilitators are prepared to interrupt meetings or discussions when necessary in order to realign the team with the meeting's goal, refocus on the agenda, and help the team improve its productivity.

Naturally, active participation is very important during virtual meetings. But how can a facilitator make sure everyone is participating when the meeting is being held over the phone or via a videoconference? The key is to listen closely and be patient with the team's progress.

As a facilitator, you should give team members an opportunity to express their thoughts without being influenced by any input from you. Save *your* ideas for last. You may even want to put your contributions in a "what if. . . ?" form.

In high-performing virtual teams, team members often take on a facilitation role as needed, depending on the meeting objectives. Everyone takes responsibility for keeping the group on track, ensuring that time is well-managed, and ensuring that meeting objectives are being met.

To reinforce the shared nature of the meeting, arrange for different people to lead parts of the session. If appropriate, you can even ask team members to rotate the facilitator role itself. The facilitation tips shown in Table 7.1 will help build a collaborative v-meeting environment.

Table 7.1 Tips for Leaders/Facilitators

Be sure that . . .	How?
Everyone understands the objectives and agenda for the meeting.	• Check in at the beginning of the meeting to ensure team members know the goals. • Ask people whether they have any questions. • Ask them what they would like to accomplish during the meeting.
All people are treated with respect.	• If there is a disagreement between individuals, de-personalize the conflict by shifting the emphasis from the people to the issue. • If there are disagreements, start any discussion by highlighting the common ground or areas of agreement before pointing out the disagreement.
All ideas are treated with respect.	• Remember, even the craziest ideas deserve to be heard. Before discussing an idea, make sure that it was understood by the whole team and try to identify the value in the idea (what you like about it, its advantages, etc. Stretch for positives if you have to!). • Discuss concerns by approaching them from a problem-solving perspective.
Everyone in the meeting has some airtime.	• Make sure everyone knows he or she will be expected to contribute. • Give people time to think about their responses. • Singling out one person to answer a question has an upside and a downside—people know you are paying attention to them, but they really may not have an answer to your question, so be careful how you use this technique.

(continued overleaf)

Table 7.1 (*Continued*)

Be sure that . . .	How?
Everyone is clear about the team's next steps.	• At the end of each meeting, review the decisions made and decide on the team's next steps. Reinforce what's decided by sending out a summary statement to the group as a follow-up to the session.

V-Meeting Checklist

In order to make the most of your v-meetings, you must lay out what will happen before, during, and after the meeting. Table 7.2 summarizes the key elements of effective meeting management by outlining the steps that need to be taken at every stage.

Building a V-Meeting Agenda

The agenda is the key to virtual meeting success. It should be set and distributed electronically as far in advance of the meeting as possible so team members can begin planning how they will contribute.

When creating a meeting agenda, start by identifying the main goal or purpose of the meeting. Next, draft a list of potential agenda items—including a list of items to cover, follow-up items from the team's last meeting, and items suggested by attendees (from previous meetings or via email in preparation for the meeting). Once the list of agenda items is compiled, prioritize it and then determine how much time will need to be spent discussing each item and how long the meeting as a whole will be.

If your time frame is fixed, ensure that you do not have too many agenda items to cover. Be aware that items requiring decision making or problem solving will take longer than items that only require information giving or gathering. And keep in mind, the larger your team, the longer decision making and problem solving will take.

Table 7.2 Virtual Meeting Outline

Before Meeting	During Meeting	After Meeting
• Develop agenda/ allot times. • Determine who needs to attend and invite participants, giving them as much advance notice as possible. • Distribute agenda (and any necessary background materials) so team members can prepare. • Secure appropriate technologies. • Know your audience and anticipate discussions in advance if possible. • Prepare your own presentation/key points.	• Start on time. • Introduce people who don't know each other. • Make sure everyone has the agenda. • Review priorities. • Set ground rules for decision making (consensus, discussion with leader decision, majority vote?). • Follow agenda. • Facilitate discussion, interaction. • Listen with respect to all points of view. • Assign action items/ responsibilities. • Track decisions made. • Take notes/minutes. • Summarize decisions/action items. • Set date for next meeting, if needed. • Close on or before the scheduled end time.	• Distribute notes/minutes promptly. • Complete your own action items. • Follow up on action items. • Ask for feedback on the meeting's effectiveness.

Keeping Virtual Meetings on Track

Now that you have structured a meeting agenda, how do you keep everyone on track during the meeting to ensure that all your objectives are accomplished? First, be up-front with your team. Tell them that staying on track is everyone's responsibility. Next, be well-prepared. And finally, use process intervention when necessary.

Process intervention occurs when the facilitator, team leader, or a team member interrupts the meeting or a certain discussion to refocus the participants and/or to rebalance group interactions. The goal is to help team members achieve their desired outcomes by keeping them on track and to balance participation with results. Be supportive when you intervene and always start with the most subtle and least threatening method of intervention. For example, during a conversation about a topic that is clearly tangential to the planned agenda, share your observation that, although it may be interesting, the current discussion is taking the group off the meeting agenda. Then ask the team whether they would like to continue with this discussion (with the understanding that they may not have time for the planned items) or if they'd rather "table it" and take it up at a later time.

Three key practices help meeting facilitators determine when an intervention is required and what type of intervention should be used.

The first is *observation*. Pay close attention to the flow of the discussion. Are the comments and issues being raised aligned with the stated agenda? Also, attend to the team's or a team member's interactions by focusing on behaviors and patterns. Keep in mind that you won't have the luxury of being able to see the meeting participants' body language or other visual cues. Therefore, it is particularly important to keep up with the level of participation of individual members and to listen carefully to their tone and choice of words.

The next step is the *diagnosis*. Is the topic something the team should discuss even though it is not on the agenda? Is there enough time to take a "side trip" or is sticking with the planned agenda more important? Here you also analyze the participant's behavior to determine whether it requires attention. For example, is the behavior getting in the way of team productivity or progress? Are team members staying focused on the goal and agenda?

Finally, based on your observation and diagnosis, *choose the appropriate intervention* technique for the team. This might include asking a question to assess a point of view, refocusing the team toward a goal, or summarizing a point under discussion.

To illustrate how different interventions might work, Table 7.3 shows strategies that Ted, a high-performing virtual team leader, uses when his meetings get off track or when disagreements pop up.

Table 7.3 Intervention Techniques

When the Meeting Gets Off Track	
Speaking for yourself	"I think it would be helpful if we got back on the agenda."
Speaking to the individual(s)	"That sounds like an interesting issue, Don, and we do need to resolve it, but it's not on today's agenda."
Speaking to the team	"The team seems to be moving off our stated agenda."
When There Is Disagreement	
Speaking for yourself	"As I understand it, the two choices that we are discussing are..."
Speaking to the individual(s)	"Pete and Julie, you seem to be in disagreement. Can you each state your position on this issue—and we'll all listen to both of you?"
Speaking to the team	"Only two people seem to be engaged in this discussion, where does everyone else stand?"

Three common situations require intervention to keep a virtual meeting on track—*staying on time, ending a long, drawn-out discussion,* and *managing conflict.* Table 7.4 lists suggestions on how to intervene in each situation.

Table 7.4 Strategies to Deal with Common Virtual Meeting Challenges

Topic	Situation	Intervention
Staying on Time	The team has a lot to cover in the agenda, but they seem too bogged down in details and frequently veer off into other topics.	Invoke the "keep focused" ground rule: Suggest someone capture items that need to be pursued, but are not the focal points for this meeting.
	The team continues to veer off.	Specifically re-focus on the particular topic/agenda item: "I'd just like to remind you that we are currently discussing the team budget, so please hold discussion on other topics until we get to them."
	The discussion of a given topic has continued for some time, and you are running out of time for the item.	Attempt closure of item: "Team, we have ten minutes remaining for this item. We need to re-focus. What do we still need to discuss to conclude this item?" "We are almost out of time, but there appears to be more discussion required. Is that true?" Follow up a yes response to this query with, "What do you need in order to close on this item?" or "Why are we unable to close on this item?"

Table 7.4 (*Continued*)

Topic	Situation	Intervention
	The item is truly important and just wasn't given sufficient time for the necessary discussion and action.	Give participants a choice on how they spend their meeting time: "Is this item more important than the remaining items on the agenda and, if so, when will we address the other items?" *Note*: The answer should *not* be to prolong the meeting so that all items can be discussed.
Never-Ending Discussion	Information barriers exist. Sometimes a discussion will not come to closure because of insufficient, inaccurate or unreliable information.	Follow the same guidelines under "Staying on Time." There may not be enough valid information available to warrant moving forward on the item, in which case the team should hold the item for another meeting. If the remainder of the meeting is dependent on the completion of this item, then reschedule the meeting with action items to ensure that participants bring whatever is required next time.
Conflict: Personal Attacks	An individual is harshly criticized. A group member takes "shots" at other team members. For example, let's say Bill is taking "shots" at Joe.	Apply gentle humor: Say nothing on the first occurrence unless you are sure that it was intentional, or make light of the first occurrence: "I hope that comment isn't an indication that we need armor for this meeting."

(*continued overleaf*)

Table 7.4 (*Continued*)

Topic	Situation	Intervention
	Bill makes another remark.	Restate the ground rules. Say to Bill, "We welcome all ideas and comments that build or clarify ideas but not negativity."
	Once again, Bill directs another sarcastic or belittling remark at Joe.	Confront Bill directly. Use firm words and a supportive tone: "Bill this is not the first time that you have targeted Joe with your remarks. Please stop." Then redirect him with "What is the concern you have with the issue/idea? How would you modify it to improve it?"

Dealing with Other Common Challenges

In addition to this trio of "derailers," there are three other important challenges v-meeting facilitators must be aware of to ensure that meetings are a good use of time for their team members. They are *scheduling, communication,* and *matching technology to task*. Let's focus for a moment on each one.

Scheduling

One of the most common difficulties is finding a meeting time that works well for all team members, especially for global virtual teams whose members may span multiple time zones. Team members we interviewed often complained of having to work longer hours—working at 10:00 p.m. or even getting up at 3:00 a.m.—to accommodate their virtual teams.

Zeller discussed her team's challenge with finding times that were convenient for members across multiple time zones. She recommended rotating meeting times so that the same team members do not always get stuck working at undesirable hours. If you are a global virtual team, this is one way you can alleviate a significant burden on team members.

Communication

Another common challenge on cross-cultural virtual teams is communication. Language barriers can pose big problems, and these problems are exacerbated when people are not face-to-face. Some virtual teams have warm-ups, or informal (non-work-related) conversations, at the beginning of meetings. These warm-ups help team members transition from their native language and listen to one another to become accustomed to accents or unfamiliar pronunciations. They also allow people to get to know each other, which helps build trust within the team.

A virtual team we worked with had several members for whom English was a second language, which often inhibited communication during teleconferences. The team leader asked each team member to share a brief story or update in English at the beginning of each meeting, which had positive results. Other virtual teams may use native translators to help clarify key messages and ensure that any cultural nuances are not lost when team members communicate with one another.

Matching Technology to the Task

Media richness researchers[1,2] believe that communication media can be classified by their level of "richness" based on certain factors: namely, their capacity for feedback, the number of cues used, and how personal they are. Specifically, on a continuum of richness, face-to-face communication would be classified as the most "rich," followed by video, telephone, instant messaging, email, and bulletin boards. As a result of differences in degree of richness, individuals favor certain media depending on the nature of the task.

Some virtual teams unwittingly choose certain technologies for communication and collaboration that hurt rather than help them reach their objectives. When making these decisions, consider how much collaboration will be necessary to successfully complete the task or objective and then determine the appropriate level of "richness." For example, email, which is a one-way medium, is best for tasks that require little collaboration. On the other hand, when teams need to solve complex problems or make decisions, technology such as videoconferencing or collaborative software tools, such as Hewlett-Packard's Halo or Cisco's TelePresence, are best.

One global virtual team in our study attempted to use emails to make decisions and solve problems. However, they found that trying to do so led to delayed and low quality decisions. Conversely, consider a global manufacturing team that we worked with that was deliberate about selecting the most appropriate technology for each task they undertook. They used videoconferencing and teleconferences when making important decisions or solving problems. In between v-meetings, they used email and instant messaging to keep one another updated and to pass on important information. The team met in person once or twice a year to discuss the team's strategy and build relationships with one another.

Table 7.5 provides guidelines for matching the right technology to your virtual team's objective.

In summary, Table 7.6 outlines do's and don'ts for successful virtual team meetings.

Conclusion

Many virtual team leaders neglect to properly plan out their team meetings. In some cases, leaders are simply too busy to prepare for and follow up after their meetings. In other situations, they don't have the knowledge and skills to run a successful team discussion.

Table 7.5 Selecting the Most Appropriate Technology

Objective/Task	Recommended Technology
Share information or ideas	Email or telephone; blogs
Provide updates ·	Email or telephone; blogs
Generate ideas	Teleconferences or videoconferencing; collaborative software (to allow for "brainstorming" and enable team members to "build" on the ideas of others) Email or telephone (when the focus is on the exchange of individual suggestions)
Solve problems	Teleconferences or videoconferencing; collaborative software
Make complex decisions	Teleconferences or videoconferencing; collaborative software
Building relationships, negotiating, or gaining commitment	Face-to-face (if possible)
Resolve conflicts	Face-to-face (if possible)

Table 7.6 Summary of Virtual Meeting "Do's" and "Don'ts"

Do	Don't
• Ensure that all stakeholders essential to achieving the meeting's goals can attend. Otherwise, reschedule it. • Consider rotating the meeting time to accommodate those participants in different time zones. • Prepare an agenda that outlines the meeting goals. • Cancel a regularly scheduled meeting if you feel time could be better spent elsewhere.	• Let meetings become "habit." • Hold a meeting if you can't clearly answer the question, "What is the purpose and expected outcome?" • Attempt to cover more than five specific items per meeting. • Hold a meeting if any stakeholders essential to the meeting objectives cannot attend.

(continued overleaf)

Table 7.6 (Continued)

Do	Don't
• Send a meeting reminder with the agenda, any necessary materials, and information on technology that may be used at least three days before the meeting.	• Assume team members are clear about their roles and the meeting objectives.
• Ask team members who are not speaking to put their phones on mute.	• Continuously hold "marathon" meetings without any small-group brainstorming or breaks.
• Ensure everyone participates.	• Start late.
• Eliminate distractions—ask people to turn off all cell phones and BlackBerries and to avoid using email and IM during virtual meetings.	• Tackle critical topics at the end of the meeting.
	• Let the meeting get off track by discussing details of an action item that aren't relevant to the meeting's goals.
• Document decisions and next steps.	
• Summarize at the end—review decisions, next steps, and accountabilities.	
• Send copies of meeting notes to all participants following the meeting.	
• Periodically gather feedback on how your virtual meetings could be more meaningful.	

Unfortunately, we have witnessed numerous examples where poor meeting management led to virtual team performance issues. The positive news is that with a little work team leaders can improve the quality and value of their v-meetings. By properly planning, intervening when necessary to keep the team on track, and selecting the appropriate communication and collaboration technologies to match the team's tasks, leaders can facilitate high-impact virtual meetings and successfully lead from a distance.

The Bottom Line

It is critical that virtual team leaders focus on the practices that support effective virtual communication and meeting management. The most effective leaders understand the unique factors inherent in leading and communicating from a distance and take the necessary steps to ensure they are able to lead their teams successfully.

Conclusion: Six Lessons for Successful Virtual Teams

As you've gone through each chapter, we hope you've learned some tactics you can put into practice today and in the future. Now we'd like to ask you to step back and take a broader look at some "big picture" principles.

The survey results that inspired this book point to six general lessons for successful virtual teams. These broader themes relate (sometimes directly and other times indirectly) to the topics that we've covered. They are summarized below.

Lesson 1: Focus on People Issues

Essentially, successful teaming depends largely on the effective interaction of team members. And because an inherent lack of human contact comes with the territory with virtual teams, they must compensate by finding ways to support team spirit, trust, and productivity.

As we've observed in earlier chapters, approaches to virtual teamwork are different from those used for conventional teams, and such matters of communication and culture—the so-called "people issues"—take on a heightened relevance to the success of these teams.

What are the warning signs that your virtual team's people issues need more attention? Do team members work independently and fail to collaborate or effectively interact with other members of the team? Or have you noticed that an "us versus them" mentality has developed between locations or subgroups?

What can you do to improve communication and relationships among team members? We suggest eight possible actions:

1. Develop a team web page where virtual team members can share information and get to know one another.
2. Create ways for team members to interact and communicate informally (virtual water cooler).
3. Build a collective "resource bank" to share experiences.
4. Find ways to "spotlight" team members.
5. Send newsletters or updates to the team.
6. Create ways to virtually celebrate successes as a team.
7. Partner team members at different locations and rotate these periodically.
8. Invite thought leaders or speakers to engage with the team, particularly on relevant topics or ideas.

Lesson 2: No Trust, No Team

Trust is the second of three factors that impact virtual team success. Task-based trust is one of the strongest determinants of high performance and one of the factors that differentiates top-performing teams.

As we've said, in virtual teams trust seems to develop more readily at the task level than at the interpersonal level. There are four warning signs that your team's members are suffering from low levels of trust. They include:

1. Team members do not refer to themselves as "we."
2. Team members do not appear to know one another very well.
3. Team members are openly negative.
4. Team members do not regard the commitments of others as credible.

When faced with this situation, our research found that team members can build trust when:

- Teams meet face-to-face at least once early on in the team's formation.
- Communication is truly open.
- Members feel empowered to make and act on decisions.
- Conflicts are managed and not avoided.
- The team leader models and reinforces these positive behaviors.

Lesson 3: "Soft" Skills Are Essential

The presence of "soft" skills makes a difference in virtual team performance. We found that virtual teams who have been through team building and interpersonal skill development perform better than those that have not. Therefore, soft skills do matter. Unfortunately, despite the strong link between training and virtual team performance, many organizations do not make this important investment.

Another all-too-common practice, selecting team members based solely on their technical skills, only increases the likelihood you will have to deal with this performance barrier. The obvious solution is to include a demonstrated competence in areas like conflict management and collaboration in the selection criteria.

The reality, of course, is that team leaders often don't get to pick who will be on their teams. In some cases, team members do not have the necessary interpersonal skills to be successful. In these situations we recommend:

- Team-building sessions—Ideally conducted at an initial or subsequent face-to-face team meeting, the team-building session will help team members get to know each other better, strengthen working relationships, and create team momentum that can enhance team effectiveness.

- Needs assessments and skill development—Assess development needs for team members and team leaders and work on building and strengthening skills focused on these areas. This can be done through training, on-the-job assignments, and other developmental activities.

- Repeat—Continuously reassess and monitor team interaction and team needs.

Lesson 4: Watch Out For Performance Peaks

Virtual teams that have been working together for more than three years tend to be more successful than teams working together for less time. However, be aware that in some virtual teams performance tends to peak after approximately one year and then declines. While high-performing virtual teams avoid this problem by implementing strategies to overcome this peak and subsequent decline, less-effective teams are not able to do so. Therefore it's important to look out for warning signs that your virtual team may be approaching its performance peak.

When you see the warning signs of a post-peak performance decline—team members get along well but do not produce results, there is an apparent lack of clarity or direction, team members do not commit adequate time to the team—there are four actions you can take:

1. Clearly define team roles and accountabilities to minimize frustration and misunderstandings that can damage morale and derail productivity.

2. Review team processes regularly (collaboration, decision making, and problem solving).

3. Periodically examine the level of team performance. Collect feedback from various stakeholders to assess the team's performance.

4. Based on the outcomes, identify barriers to high performance, as well as steps that can be taken to overcome these barriers. Ensure that team success factors are retained.

Lesson 5: Create a "High-Touch" Environment

Electronic technology has made virtual teaming possible, but it is not a perfect substitute for human interaction. One of the greatest performance barriers is the inability to replicate a "high-touch" environment in a virtual setting. While meeting face-to-face requires time and expense, virtual teams that invest in one or two such meetings per year perform better overall than those that do not.

Poor communication, a lack of engagement, and a lack of attention during virtual meetings are a few of the warning signs that a high-touch environment is not being achieved. There are, however, several things that can be done to reverse this situation:

- Leverage synchronous tools (such as instant messaging) to increase spontaneous communication.
- Use tools such as electronic bulletin boards to create a sense of shared space.
- Carefully choose communication technologies that are most appropriate to the specific task:
  - Avoid using conference calls when information could be distributed via email or intranet posting.
  - Remember, email is good for simple information sharing, while conference calls are better suited for interactive sharing of ideas or plans.
- Develop a communication strategy but re-examine these processes over time.
- Make wider use of videoconferencing. Our survey data suggests that teams that use video technology perform better in general than those that do not.

When trying to achieve a high touch virtual environment, it is important to watch out for "technology overkill." Teams that reported using a high number of communication methods tended to be among the low performers, as they were likely using too many technologies with minimal impact.

Lesson 6: Virtual Team Leadership Matters

Leadership is the most important factor for the success of virtual teams. Our study and other research shows that leadership does, in fact, have a statistically significant correlation with higher performance on virtual teams. To be effective, team leaders in a virtual environment must be especially sensitive to interpersonal communication and cultural factors to overcome the limitations of long-distance teaming.

The warning signs of an ineffective team leader include: (1) the team isn't meeting its performance objectives and deliverables are delayed or of poor quality; (2) relationships between the team members and the leader are damaged; (3) the leader is not clear about the team's direction or purpose; and (4) the team leader pays more attention to members who are at his or her location or with whom he or she has the best relationships.

Organizations can avoid this problem by selecting team leaders who not only have the necessary technical skills but who also have the soft skills required to effectively lead in a virtual environment. According to our research, the critical interpersonal characteristics of an effective virtual team leader include communication and influencing skills, the ability to consistently motivate others, the ability to build relationships, and the ability to coach and develop others.

Another leadership quality—being committed to seeing outcomes through from start to finish—plays a prominent role in distinguishing high- from medium-performing teams.

If you're a team leader, it's not easy to learn that you may be the cause of your team's poor performance. But should you find yourself faced with this challenge, there are several things you can do to improve performance:

- Set clear goals and direction, and revisit these as priorities shift.
- Engage team members in development of strategies.
- Provide time early on for team building and coordinate periodic face-to-face meetings.
- Find ways to ensure that team members feel included.
- Provide timely feedback to team members. Be responsive and accessible.
- Emphasize common interests and values and reinforce cooperation and trust.
- Create a system to easily integrate new team members.
- Teach the importance of conflict resolution.
- Celebrate team achievements and successes.
- Focus on the four elements of successful teamwork (relationships, accountability, motivation, and purpose/process).

Closing Thoughts

Organizations that get it right know that virtual teams and co-located teams are as different as apples and oranges. But unfortunately, too many organizations have yet to catch on to this critical truth.

We've seen plenty of well-intentioned companies fail because they treat their virtual teams the same way they treat their co-located teams. And then there are the organizations that start virtual teams on a whim without the proper planning or follow-up—never a recipe for success.

Many companies think that if they have the right technology their virtual teams can't possibly fail. As a result, they neglect other interpersonal and structural factors necessary for virtual teamwork.

Technology is, of course, only a tool. While it's important for virtual teams, our research shows that it's a prerequisite rather than a differentiator. Technological advancements will certainly continue to impact how people collaborate and work together from a distance. As technologies that bridge distance and help compensate for the lack of face-to-face interaction continue to develop, virtual teamwork will become much easier and more efficient.

Organizations frequently set up virtual teams and task forces to address particular business needs. However, as mentioned before, they jump in without really understanding what they're getting themselves into. By coupling better planning with the right mix of communication technologies, they could dramatically improve their chances for success.

It's important that organizations ensure they have the proper structure and systems in place to support virtual teamwork. For example, in addition to the technology, leaders need to have the appropriate skills to lead from a distance. There also need to be recognition and reward systems in place to reinforce virtual collaboration. Even if virtual teams have all of the appropriate systems and structural issues taken care of, it's imperative that they build trust and focus on the people issues that are fundamental to success.

The Economist Intelligence Unit's *Foresight 2020: Economic, Industry, and Corporate Trends* report[1] outlines five key trends for the future. Two of these trends, globalization and knowledge management, are particularly relevant to virtual teamwork. With the continued proliferation of global trends such as outsourcing, cross-organizational collaboration, and joint ventures, virtual collaboration is likely to increase exponentially in the future. And the shift from production to knowledge work will also impact how employees do their jobs.

While we may be a long way from creating organizations that are entirely virtual, the workplace of the future will likely look very different. As Townsend asserts,[2] "This new workplace will be unrestrained by geography, time, and organizational boundaries; it will be a virtual workplace where productivity, flexibility, and collaboration will reach unprecedented new levels."

As companies continue to expand their global reach, they will rely heavily on virtual teams to achieve business objectives. The good news is that these teams can be extremely successful. However, they *must* put forth the required investments of time and resources to ensure that they can perform to the best of their abilities. Based on our research and experiences working with virtual teams, organizations that take the necessary steps to successfully launch them and to ensure that there are processes in place to assess their performance experience much greater virtual team success over time.

The Bottom Line

While virtual teams should not be viewed as a panacea for organizations, when properly implemented and supported, they can be a competitive advantage.

OnPoint's Global Virtual Team Study

Study Background

A new study conducted by OnPoint surveyed forty-eight virtual teams across industries to identify specific practices associated with the most successful virtual teams. The focus of this study was not to compare face-to-face teams with virtual teams but to understand what factors differentiate high-performing virtual teams so that companies can implement high-impact strategies to make virtual teams more productive.

The population for this study was intact virtual teams, or teams whose members work together interdependently, are geographically dispersed, and who do not regularly meet face-to-face. If a team met the following criteria, they were eligible for the study:

Eligibility Criteria

❑ Does the team rely on one another to get work done (that is, they are interdependent)?

❑ Are members of the team geographically dispersed?

❑ Do at least one-third of the team members work in different locations?

❑ Are there between three and thirty team members?

Study Methodology

The primary method of data collection was a virtual team inventory that was administered to 427 team members and leaders between May and August 2008. In addition, third-party feedback was collected from ninety-nine key stakeholders (individuals who are very familiar with the teams, such as internal customers or the team leader's manager) to objectively assess team performance. Finally, we conducted forty-five telephone interviews with team members and team leaders to better understand their experiences and challenges.

The Online Virtual Team Inventory assessed six dimensions of virtual team performance, including: Results, Communication, Team Motivation, Interpersonal Relationships, Collaboration, and Purpose and Roles. The overall reliability of the virtual team inventory was very high (α = .95). The Team Performance Assessment, completed by stakeholders, contained selected items from the team assessment primarily focused on outcomes, including an overall assessment of team and leader effectiveness.

Team Demographics

The majority of teams (52 percent) had six to twelve members. One-quarter of teams had thirteen to twenty members (see Figure A.1).

Figure A.1 Team Makeup

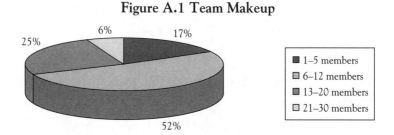

25% 6% 17%

1–5 members
6–12 members
13–20 members
21–30 members

52%

Just under half of those studied had been working together for one to three years, whereas roughly the same percentage of teams had less than one year of tenure (see Figure A.2).

Figure A.2 Tenure on the Team

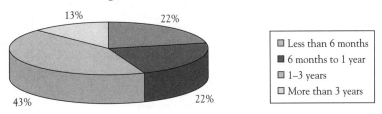

Nearly half of team members reported being on only one virtual team, another third reporting being on two or three virtual teams, and the remaining team members were on more than three teams (Figure A.3).

Figure A.3 Virtual Team Memberships

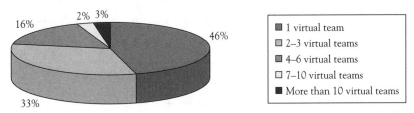

Forty-one percent of the virtual teams had never participated in any skill development or team-building sessions (Figure A.4).

Figure A.4 Skill Development or Team-Building Activities

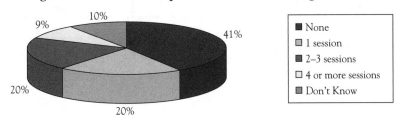

About half of the teams participating were cross-functional in nature. Title, level, and function of participants are shown in Table A.1.

Table A.1 Title, Level, and Function of Participants in the Study

Title	Percentage of Responses
Other	35%
Manager	22%
Director	14%
Vice president	15%
Partner	8%
Supervisor	3%
Department head	2%
CEO	1%
Level	Percentage of Responses
Individual contributor	44%
Fist-line manager	28%
Manager of manager	14%
Business/functional manager	8%
Other	6%
Function	Percentage of Responses
IT	37%
Sales	13%
HR/Personnel	12%
Other	12%
R&D	11%
Accounting/Finance	5%
Materials/Management/Purchasing	3%
Operations	3%
Marketing/Advertising	2%
Engineering	2%

Half of team members reported meeting virtually once a week or more often; 18 percent met several times a month; and the remaining teams met once per month or less frequently (see Figure A.5).

Figure A.5 Meeting Frequency

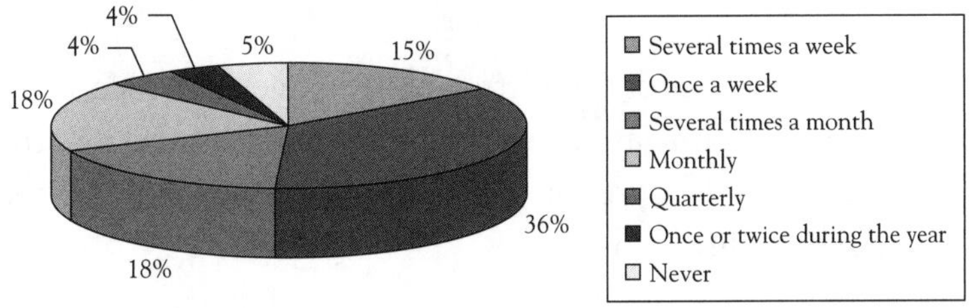

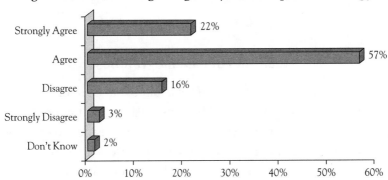

The vast majority of team members felt they had the proper technology to work together; however, most relied most frequently on email and the telephone (Figure A.6).

Figure A.6 Percent Agreeing They Had Proper Technology

Forty-three percent of team members reported meeting face-to-face only once or twice a year. Approximately 20 percent reported never having a face-to-face meeting (Figure A.7).

Figure A.7 Frequency of Face-to-Face Meetings

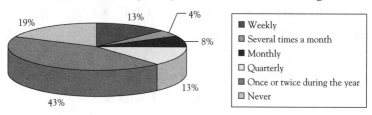

19%   13%   4%

8%

13%

43%

- Weekly
- Several times a month
- Monthly
- Quarterly
- Once or twice during the year
- Never

While 20 percent of the virtual teams never met face-to-face, 35 percent had an initial in-person meeting within the first thirty days and another 19 percent had met within the first thirty-one to sixty days (Figure A.8).

Figure A.8 Timing of Face-to-Face Meetings

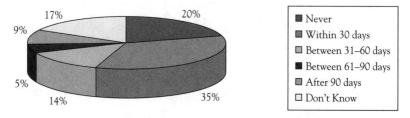

17%   20%

9%

5%

14%   35%

- Never
- Within 30 days
- Between 31–60 days
- Between 61–90 days
- After 90 days
- Don't Know

Team Leader Demographics

Team leaders were frequently direct managers of team members and in most cases had relationships with team members that spanned one to three years. Many leaders needed to balance managing their direct reports, as well as people who were on their virtual team who either reported to their peers or who were their own peers, which was difficult when leading from a distance.

Across most teams (84 percent), team leadership did not change. However, 18 percent of team members believed that rotating leadership rather than having one permanent leader could enhance their performance (see Figure A.9).

Figure A.9 Team Leadership Changes

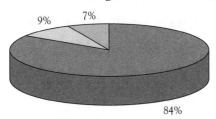

9%   7%

84%

- The team leader does not typically change
- Team leadership rotates periodically
- This team does not have a formal leader

The majority of team members (58 percent) had direct reporting relationships with their team leaders. More than 75 percent of team members reported having known their team leader three years or less. Forty percent shared a physical space (building/campus) with their team leader, while the rest were in different regions or countries (Table A.2).

Table A.2 Length of Time Worked with Leader

How Long Known Leader	*Percentage of Responses*
1 to 3 years	47%
Less than 1 year	30%
More than 6 years	13%
4 to 6 years	10%
Relationship with Leader	*Precentage of Responses*
My direct manager	58%
Report to leader for this team only	20%
My peer	19%
Other	3%
Location Relative to Leader	*Percentage of Responses*
Local (same building or campus)	40%
National (same country)	24%
Regional (same or adjacent state)	18%
Global (in a different country)	16%
Other	2%

Criteria for Identifying Top-Performing Teams

In order to identify differences between high- and lower-performing teams, we used the following approach to objectively define team performance and develop a Performance Index by classifying teams as Highly Effective, Effective, and Less Effective:

1. Team members, leaders, and stakeholders rated the overall effectiveness of the teams. For each team, ratings were averaged to produce one score representing overall team effectiveness.

2. To create a more robust measure of performance for each team, the overall average of the Team Results Dimension (see Figure A.10) were combined with the overall team effectiveness score to assess each team on specific outcomes related to performance. Regression analysis showed that the items in the Team Results Dimension were most predictive of overall performance, which supported this approach.

Figure A.10 Team Results Dimension

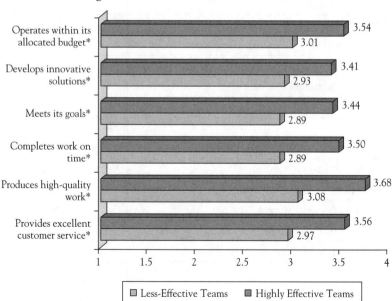

*Indicates a statistically significant difference between less-effective and highly effective teams.

3. Based on these data points, a Performance Index was created, and all forty-eight teams were classified into three groups according to their level of effectiveness. The overall performance differences were statistically significant between less effective, moderately effective, and highly effective teams.

The graph in Figure A.11 displays the results of the average scores for each of the performance dimensions assessed in the online survey across all virtual teams.

Figure A.11 Performance Dimension

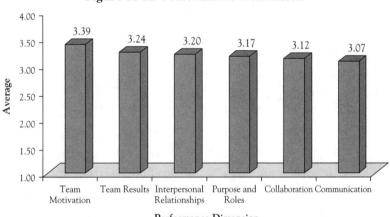

Dimensions are computed on a 4-point rating scale with 1 = Strongly Disagree and 4 = Strongly Agree

The highest-rated items, across performance dimensions (on a 4-point rating scale), are shown in Table A.3.

What Factors Impact Team Effectiveness?

Our study looked at different factors that might impact virtual team performance. First, team tenure seemed to be associated with overall virtual team effectiveness (all ratings are on a 5-point rating scale ranging from Poor to Outstanding). Differences in effectiveness by team tenure were statistically significant

Table A.3 Highest-Rated Items

Item	Average
Are willing to put in extra effort to get work done	3.48
Produces high-quality work	3.39
Demonstrates a high level of initaitive	3.32
Help one antoher achieve team goals/objectives	3.31
Are willing to assume leadership responsibiilty when appropriate	3.31
Receive the necessary feedback to enhance their contributions to the team	2.90
Involve one another in decisions appropriately	2.99
Have determined the most appropriate ways for the team to communicate	3.00
Have a shared process for decision making/problem solving	3.01
Have clear roles and responsibilities	3.02

($p = .003$). Teams of more than three years had higher effectiveness ratings than those together for less than six months, six months to one year, and one to three years. Thus, teams with more than three years tenure had the highest scores when compared to the other tenure levels (see Figure A.12).

Next, we looked at whether the frequency of team membership changes had any relationship on virtual team performance (Figure A.13). Overall, differences in effectiveness by frequency of membership changes were statistically significant ($p = .000$). Teams whose membership never changed had higher scores than those whose membership changed every few months, those whose changed several times a month, or those that changed less frequently than every few months.

We also examined whether virtual teams who had more face-to-face interaction performed better than those teams that did not. Overall, differences in effectiveness by frequency of face-to-face meetings were statistically significant ($p = .003$).

Specifically, teams who met weekly had significantly higher scores than those who met monthly (see Figure A.14).

Figure A.12 Tenure of the Teams vs. Effectiveness

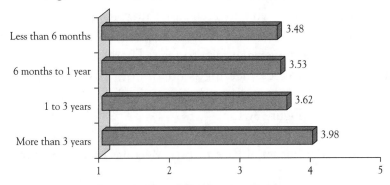

Figure A.13 Relationship Between Meeting Frequency and Effectiveness

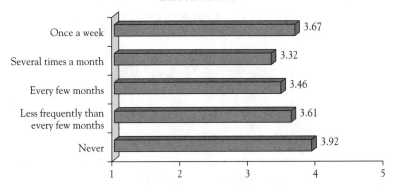

Figure A.14 Relationship Between Frequency of Face-to-Face Meetings and Performance

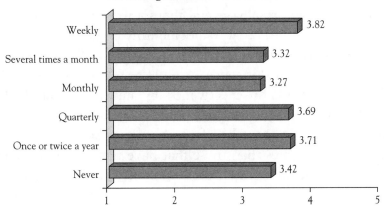

We also wanted to see whether the timing of the initial face-to-face meeting had an impact on virtual team performance. Overall, differences in effectiveness by timing of initial face-to-face meetings were statistically significant (p = .027). Specifically, teams who met within thirty to ninety days and those who met after ninety days had significantly higher scores than those who never met face-to-face. Therefore, while having an initial face-to-face meeting is important, it is less important whether this happens within the first month or the first two or three months (Figure A.15).

Figure A.15 Impact of Face-to-Face Meetings on Performance

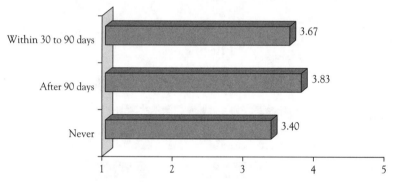

So, while face-to-face meetings matter, we also wondered whether the frequency of v-meetings had any impact on virtual team performance. Differences in effectiveness by frequency of virtual meetings were statistically significant (p = .016) such that teams who met virtually several times a week had significantly higher scores than those who met monthly (Figure A.16).

Organizations invest in team building and skill development to enhance the performance of their teams. Does it pay off? Overall, differences in effectiveness by amount of team building/skill development were statistically significant (p = .002). Specifically, teams that had four or more sessions had significantly higher scores than those that have not had any sessions and those that have only had one session. Teams that had two to three sessions also scored significantly higher than those who have not had any sessions (Figure A.17).

Figure A.16 Impact of Meeting Frequency

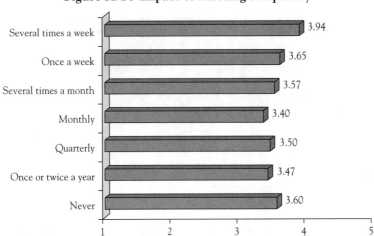

Figure A.17 Impact of Team Building and Skill Development

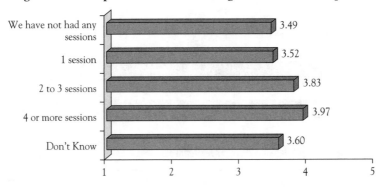

Team Leader Findings

Leaders of high-performing teams were rated the highest by team members and also provided the highest self-rating on overall effectiveness, followed by medium- and then low-performing teams, respectively. There were significant differences in team member ratings of leaders between high- and low-performing teams (p = .001) (Figure A.18).

Figure A.18 Team Member Ratings of Leaders

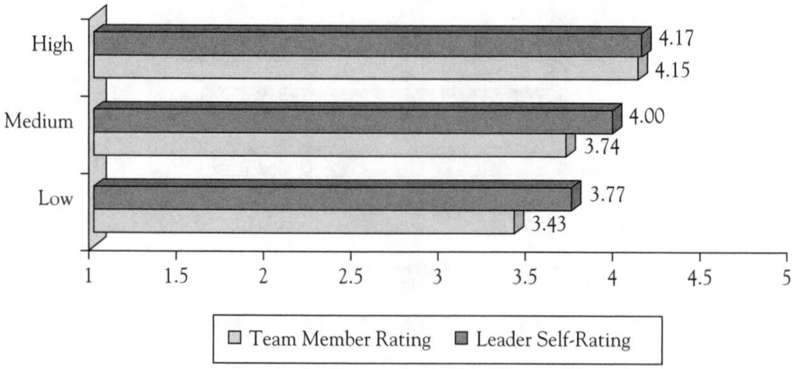

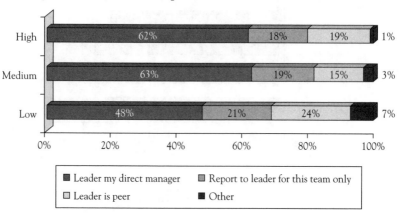

Low-performing teams seem to have fewer leaders who are members' direct managers, particularly when compared to high-performing teams (see Figure A.19).

Figure A.19 Relationship of Team Members to the Leader

The length of time that team members have known leaders does not seem to vary by team performance level, as shown in Figure A.20.

Figure A.20 How Long Team Members Have Known Leaders

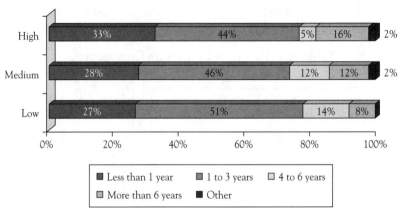

High-performing teams have more leaders who are local compared to low-performing teams, as shown in Figure A.21.

Figure A.21 Location of Leaders

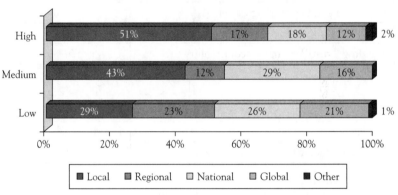

We asked virtual team members/leaders and third-party stakeholders to identify the top three most-important competencies for virtual team leaders. The results (shown in Table A.4) indicate that communication and building relationships were rated as the two most important. Results orientation and building trust/accountability were also perceived to be important.

We also asked team leaders to select the top challenges leading from a distance. Those answers are shown in Table A.5.

Table A.4 Rating of Leadership Competencies

Team Members and Leaders	
Leadership Competency	*Percentage of Responses*
Communication	60%
Building Relationships	23%
Building Trust/Personal Accoutabilty	23%
Operational/Action Planning	23%
Motivating Others	22%
Results Orientation	21%
Stakeholders	
Leadership Competency	*Percentage of Responses*
Communication	53%
Results Orientation	34%
Building Relationships	29%
Coaching and Developing Other	27%
Strateic Thinking	25%
Building Trust/Personal Accountability	24%

Table A.5 Top Challenges

Challenge	*Percentage of Responses*
Infrequent face-to-face contact as a team	43%
Lack of resources	39%
Building a collaborative atmosphere virtually	32%
Lack of time to focus on leading team	27%
Changing team/organizational priorities	23%
The team has more work than it can handle	21%
Managing poor performance	14%
Team members can only dedicate a portion of their time to the team	14%

Notes

Introduction

1. Wiener, N. (1950). *The human use of human beings*. New York: Anchor Books.
2. Handy, C. (1995, May/June). Trust and the virtual organization. *Harvard Business Review*, pp. 40–50.
3. Munamaker, J. F., Reinig, B. A., & Briggs, R. O. (2009). Principles for effective virtual teamwork. *Communications of the ACM, 52*(4).
4. Chambers, J. (2008, November). The HBR interview: Cisco sees the future. *Harvard Business Review*, pp. 72–79.
5. Conlin, M. (2008, June). The waning days of the road warrior. *BusinessWeek Online*.
6. Ibid.
7. Snyder, B. (2003, May). Teams that span time zones face new work rules. *Stanford Business Online*.

Chapter One

1. Govindarajan, V., & Gupta, A. K. (2001). *MIT Sloan Management Review, 42*(4), 63–71.

Chapter Three

1. Snyder, B. (2003, May). Quoting M. A. Neale in Teams that span time zones face new work rules. *Stanford Business*.

2. Conlin, M. (2009, June). Is there a virtual worker personality? *BusinessWeek Online*.

3. Fern, B., & Cohen, H. (2006). *Leading for employee engagement*. Bedford, NY: Performance Connections International.

4. Parker, G. M. (1996). *Team players and teamwork*. San Francisco: Pfeiffer.

Chapter Four

1. Kirkland, R. (2007, November 12). Cisco's display of strength. *Fortune*, p. 90.

2. Cascio, W. F. (2000). Managing a virtual workplace. *Academy of Management Executive, 14*(3), 81–90.

3. Zaccaro, S. J., & Bader, P. (2003). e-Leadership and the challenges of leading e-teams: Minimizing the bad and maximizing the good. *Organizational Dynamics, 31*(4), 377–387.

4. Hart, R. K., & McLeod, P. L. (2003). Rethinking team building in geographically dispersed teams. *Organizational Dynamics, 31*(4), 352–361.

5. Latane, B., Williams, K., & Harkins, S. (1979). Many hands make light the work: The causes and consequences of social loafing. *Journal of Personality and Social Psychology, 37*, 822–832.

6. Williams, K. D., Nida, S. A., Baca, L. D., & Latane, B. (1987). Social loafing and swimming: Effects of identifiability on individual and relay performance of intercollegiate swimmers. *Basic and Applied Social Psychology, 10*(1), 73–81.

7. Yeatts, D. E., & Hyten, C. (1998). *High-performing self-managed work teams: A comparison of theory to practice*. Thousand Oaks, CA: Sage.

8. Siebdraft, F., Hoegl, M., & Ernst, H. (2009). How to manage virtual teams. *MIT Sloan Management Review, 50*(4), 63–68

9. Ibid.

Chapter Five

1. Handy, C. (1995, May/June). Trust and the virtual organization. *Harvard Business Review*, pp. 40–50.
2. Canegallo, C., Ortona, G., Ottone, S., Ponzano, F., & Scacciati, F. (2008). Competition versus cooperation: Some experimental evidence. *The Journal of Socio-Economics, 37*, 18–30.
3. Monterosso, J., Ainslie, G., Toppi Mullen, P.A.-C.P., & Gault, B. (2002). The fragility of cooperation: A false feedback study of a sequential iterated prisoner's dilemma. *Journal of Economic Psychology, 23*, 437–448.
4. Patterson, G. R ., & Forgatch, M. S. (1985). Therapist behavior as a determinant for client noncompliance: A paradox for the behavior modifier. *Journal of Consulting and Clinical Psychology, 53*(6), 846–851.
5. Miller, W. R., & Rollnick, S. (2004). Talking oneself into change: Motivational interviewing, stages of change, and therapeutic process. *Journal of Cognitive Psychotherapy, 18*(4), 299–308.
6. Ibid.
7. Kirkman, B., Rosen, B., Tesluk, P., & Gibson, C. (2004, April). The impact of team empowerment on virtual team performance: The moderating role of face-to-face interaction. *Academy of Management Journal*, pp. 175–192.

Chapter Six

1. Fern, B., & Cohen, H. (2006). *Leading for employee engagement*. Bedford, NY: Performance Connections International.
2. Ibid.
3. Ibid.

Chapter Seven

1. Daft, R. L., & Lengel, R. H. (1984). Information richness: A new approach to managerial behavior and organization design. *Research in Organizational Behavior, 6,* 191–233.
2. Daft, R. L., & Lengel, R. H. (1986). Organizational information requirements, media richness and structural design. *Management Science, 32*(5), 554–571.

Conclusion

1. Economic Intelligence Unit, *The Economist.* (2006). *Foresight 2020: Economic industry and corporate trends,* pp. 1–96.
2. Townsend, A. M., DeMarie, S. M., & Hendrickson, A. R. (1998). Virtual teams: Technology and the workplace of the future. *Academy of Management Executive, 12*(3), 17–29.

About the Authors

Darleen DeRosa, Ph.D., is a managing partner at OnPoint Consulting. Darleen brings more than ten years of management consulting experience, with deep expertise in the areas of talent/succession management, executive assessment, virtual teams, and organizational assessment.

Prior to joining OnPoint Consulting, Darleen was an executive director in the assessment practice at Russell Reynolds Associates. In this role, Darleen conducted assessments of senior executives across industries and worked closely with CEOs and boards to leverage these results. Specifically, she worked with clients such as Google, Gerdau Group, Carlyle, EarthLink, Morgan Stanley, and ArQule.

Before that, Darleen served as assessment practice leader for Right Management Consultants, where she was responsible for the growth of the assessment practice for the Northeast Region. Darleen provided assessment solutions to help organizations such as Johnson & Johnson, Bayer, Merck, Rodale Publishing, FGIC, and Daiichi Sankyo, Inc., facilitate selection, succession management, and leadership development initiatives. In particular, she designed and implemented large-scale assessment projects, helped identify and develop high-potential leaders, conducted assessments of executive teams, and designed leadership development programs.

Prior to her tenure at Right Management, Darleen was a clinical researcher at the Yale University School of Medicine, where she conducted assessments and managed clinical research studies. She began her career at Southern New England Telecommunications Company (now AT&T) in human resources, where she focused on selection.

Darleen received her B.A. in psychology from the College of the Holy Cross and her M.A. and Ph.D. in social/organizational psychology from Temple University. Darleen is a member of the Society for Industrial and Organizational Psychology (SIOP), METRO, and other professional organizations. She has published book chapters and articles in journals such as *Human Resource Management*.

Darleen can be contacted at dderosa@onpointconsultingllc.com

Richard Lepsinger is president of *OnPoint* Consulting (www.onpointconsultingllc.com) and has a twenty-five year track record of success as a human resource consultant and executive. He was a founder and managing partner of Manus, a human capital consulting firm, which he grew to over $4 million in revenue and sold to Right Management Consultants in 1998. At Right, Rick was the managing vice president of the Northeast and Eastern Canadian Consulting Practice, where he was responsible to fifty-five professionals and grew the region's revenue from $7 million to $20 million.

The focus of Rick's work has been on helping organizations close the gap between strategy and execution. He has served as a consultant to leaders and management teams at Astra-Zeneca, Bayer Pharmaceuticals, Citibank, Coca-Cola Company, ConocoPhilipps, Eisai Inc., GlaxoSmithKline, Goldman Sachs, Johnson & Johnson, KPMG, Merck & Co., the NYSE Euronext, Northwestern Mutual Life, PeopleSoft, Pfizer Inc., Pitney Bowes, Prudential, Siemens Medical Systems, Subaru of America, and UBS, among others.

Rick has extensive experience in formulating and implementing strategic plans, managing change, and talent management.

He has addressed executive conferences and made presentations to leadership teams on the topics of leader effectiveness, strategy execution, managing change, performance management, 360-degree feedback and its uses, and developing and using competency models to enhance organizational performance.

Rick has co-authored or authored four books on leadership, including *Flexible Leadership: Creating Value by Balancing Multiple Challenges and Choices* (with Dr. Gary Yukl), published by Jossey-Bass; *The Art and Science of 360-Degree Feedback* (2nd ed.; with Toni Lucia), published by Pfeiffer; *The Art and Science of Competency Models* (with Toni Lucia), published by Pfeiffer, and his most recent book, *Closing the Execution Gap: How Great Leaders and Their Companies Get Results*, published by Jossey-Bass.

He is also the author of several book chapters and articles on leadership and organizational effectiveness, including "Performance Management and Decision Making" in *The Handbook of Multisource Feedback;* and "Using 360-Degree Feedback in a Talent Management System" in *The Talent Management Handbook: Creating Organizational Excellence by Identifying, Developing, and Promoting Your Best People.* "Why Integrating the Leading and Managing Roles Is Essential for Organizational Effectiveness" (with Dr. Gary Yukl) appeared in *Organizational Dynamics* and is one of their most frequently downloaded articles.

Rick can be contacted at rlepsinger@onpointconsultingllc.com.

Index